THE GAL

THE WORLD AC

The Galactic Historian
The World According to Andrew Bartzis

Copyright 2021 ©Andrew Bartzis. All rights reserved. No part of this publication, text or illustrations, may be reproduced, stored in a retrieval system or transmitted, in any form or by any means, without the prior written consent of the publisher or a license from the author.

Paperback ISBN: 978-1-7372905-1-3

Illustrations Copyright 2021 ©Martina Grubmueller.

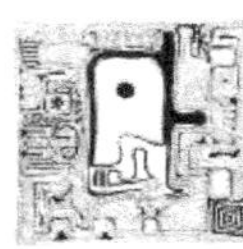
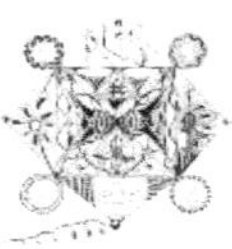

Contents

I celebrate myself, and sing myself,
And what I assume you shall assume,
For every atom belonging to me as good belongs to you.

Walt Whitman — *Leaves of Grass*

Time is a good story teller.
Celtic proverb

Foreword

I am like an atom, a nothing left in darkness,
And yet I am an identity.
They told me I had five senses to close me up,
And they enclosed my infinite brain into a narrow circle,
And sunk my heart into the Abyss...
Till all from Life was obliterated and erased.
Man has closed himself up, till he sees all things
thro' narrow chinks of his cavern.
If the doors of perception were cleansed everything
would appear to man as it is, infinite.

His Sense of Exile — William Blake

There is Something New Under the Sun

Inside this text, resides the seed of all aspects of sublime truths which many have been seeking in extremely obscure and often downright confusing sources. The old guard of spiritual gatekeepers may want to dismiss this book as more *fluff* mainly due to their earnest belief that spirituality must be an exercise in suffering, a figurative labor of love which lays the neophyte spread eagle on the ground crying out in the darkness waiting for revelations to be birthed from sacred orifices. I would invite these brethren to pause a while from the regular spiritual masturbation and self-flagellation which has characterized them for centuries and step away from the Lodges and Mystery School manuscripts and read this work because this text is a distillation of truths, we know to be correct; but presented in a way which is accessible to the profane. Save the birthing process for future incarnations.

I also speak to those with social media attention spans to consider what they lose without reading. This version of *diet spirituality* in the age of social media diatribe has been the cause of factionalism within the spiritual and holistic communities. Gone are the days when deep thought and the patience it took to realize the great truths of the Universe were a staple in spiritual practice. Google and weekend courses have replaced epiphany with participation certificates and 0.07 microsecond enlightenment. Indeed, it is said that the man who can read and does not read, has no advantage over a man who cannot read. I would invite the new-agers to stretch themselves into a space where expansion is not a hit or miss affair. Indeed, it is a wonderful thing to stretch the mind and the spirit along with the body, so please pull out the yoga mats and open your heart chakras to a new reality.

My Knowledge of the Galactic Historian

Andrew Bartzis, the Galactic Historian made himself known to me three years ago when I was, for want of a better word; *sleeping*. Many years of being a practitioner of Esoteric Philosophy as well as a mentor and teacher to students of the Eastern and Western Esoteric traditions had created a sort of spiritual burnout, where I sought refuge in the darkness of an apartment in Oakville Canada.

A choice visit to Barbados would put me into contact with the Galactic Historian and I knew instantly when I met him that this was not an individual who was a *dabbler* or another *light worker* in name only. Subsequent discussions with Andrew revealed that he was the recipient of what he called *downloads* which were at the basis of most of his teachings.

Being a natural skeptic, I had to engage in many discussions with him to realize that he was not just pirating teachings which have been leaked on the internet from truth peddlers who sell discount versions of truth in the marketplace of ignorance, but he was indeed authentic. All too often we become locked in our own limited ways of thinking which can be expanded if we allow others to see and point out our blind spots and call us out on them. This is the true dharma which escapes many of us.

In this book, our author has given us a multidimensional helicopter tour of Ontology, however this is not the kind of helicopter ride you are meant to come down from, neither does the tour end after reading this text. This text is meant to engage the reader not as a passive recipient in a one-way communication field but as an active participant in the dialogue of what makes his/her existence what it is.

There are several facets which the book covers. It covers Galactic History sliding along our history as we know it and it rails against the status quo of established ideologies. The author has meant for this to be a bumpy tour and so it is.

For those of us who, in error have mistaken the *shared illusion* which we have come to accept as the real reality — even though physics has, through evidence proven otherwise — this book will be a helpful reminder of how our attachment to this illusion is what creates the fragility in our spiritual practices and beliefs.

This hologram which binds us into this shared understanding is challenged and a new narrative is formed often quite hilariously in the text. What if we treat the hologram like a hologram? What if we treat this reality like the alternate reality we so often refer to as our dream states? What happens then, dear reader? Does society fall apart? Or do we gain permanent insight into a creation which is less confining than our collective experience.

Further, how does one express our concept of free will in a reality where we literally see what *others* want us to see and experience. This conundrum forms the basis for an argument for making this shared reality an alternate reality, that we choose to engage in consciously as opposed to the idea of *a real existence.*

This chain of questioning and internal dialogue, written in a stream of consciousness pervades this text and challenges our concept of creation. It is easy for us to believe that we were created by some arcane and powerful force which watches over us and protects us. Others believe we are in a co-creationist universe which has no will except evolution. All of these vague concepts represent really ornate ways of saying *I don't know anything, and I don't think I'm smart enough to figure it out.* If you have given up on your ability to *figure it out for yourself* and you have surrendered your intellect and dignity to the hologram then this text might anger you somewhat because it will challenge your comfort levels to wake up and start exploring meaningfully again.

This natural inquisitiveness which many of us have put to sleep is the cause of much disharmony within and without the hologram. If spiritual intellect was a river flowing directly from the mind of god then surely the end of curiosity and wonder is the stagnation of the will of god itself.

These troubling insights are explored in this text in no vague way. What Andrew has done here is become really specific with the limits of universal law, the application of it, and the consequences when it is broken.

Our concepts of karma, the universal credit system, our corporeal interfaces and the actual interactions which govern the processes of co-creation are explained in minute details.

I would personally advise readers to read this text more than once as the revelations contained can help with understanding everything from the rising gas prices in your locality to why it is you get sick.

On Secrets and Secret Societies

The value of this text is revealed in its universal application. Too often, we get caught on opposite sides of the spectrum of our understanding. Either our heads float off into the clouds of obscurity or we dig ourselves a grave in the mundane nature of the hologram. Complete awareness however requires us to have our heads in the clouds and our feet on the ground and this we have seen is the mystery of the hexagram from our venerable brothers in the Martinist order.

For a very long time, we have seen the divide which was artificially created between the *older* knowledge of the mystery schools and occult fraternities; and the new age spiritual *drive throughs* which have been producing *enlightened beings* at discount rate.

Many in the old guard of occult knowledge have looked at this development with shock, horror and quite often disgust and have refused to see that their reactions to this belies their own insecurities that their beloved practice and its significance may be coming to an end.

The world has changed and we too must change if we are to continue these great traditions.

Part of this change should be the acceptance that we do not have all the answers and that maybe, just maybe our understanding of the universal order may be flawed in many ways.

Too often our judgment of this new version of spirituality misses the mark in understanding that we should meet people where they are. We are all in this artificial matrix which this book refers to as the hologram and having ten sets of keys as opposed to one set of keys does not make one less imprisoned, if he being of an exalted nature, still cannot open the door.

My brothers and sisters, it is for this reason we need teachings such as the ones represented in this text, which seeks to transport your perspectives outside of the hologram fueled by personal bias and false light.

Our understanding of the universe must begin with our understanding that we are our own jailers and that the realization that we are self-incarcerated should prompt action.

Our author's helicopter view invites us to stop thinking in simple patterns, sowing division amongst ourselves as a distraction from the fact that *we do not know how to get out* and choose to admit, like the first step in the journey of an alcoholic, that we have a problem.

We are addicted to the hologram. We are addicted to false light and false teachings and we are addicted to the self-created dramas which plague our existence. All in the worship of illusion.

What a glorious day it would be if we decided to excavate ourselves from limiting belief systems and think wider and higher. The Galactic Historian invites you on such a journey to the realization of this goal as a self-imposed crusade out of the *holy land* of ignorance and into the realization of higher forms. This is an open invitation and one not to be dismissed for the true seekers of answers in the universal order.

David Dean Ellis DD. LL.M MBA F :.

The Unknown Philosopher

F.U.D.O.S.I

Part I

Context

Chapter 1

Reality

Hologram

Our reality here on earth is a hologram, a matrix, a simulation, a simulacrum. It's a bit pithy, and it fits in quite well with the technology-driven cognitive dystopia we can call the global narrative – the non-stop, cradle to grave, thought-womb propaganda, digital, analog, and paper — we are immersed in daily. It's in our literature, our music, our movies, our science. It's all fake, don't you know? Elon Musk says he's almost certain we live in a computer simulation. If you watch a lot of science fiction, you may have noticed it's all artificial light or darkness, very few sunny days. Why don't they ever explain what happens to consciousness in space? How does gravity affect our thoughts? If twenty-one grams leaves the body upon death, what does a weightless environment do for that other part? It's not that they don't know. They do. The disparity between what they know and what they encourage us to believe is so great now we may as well be separate species, literally separate species.

That would explain the contempt, the indifference, the empathy dislocation. Psychopathy is an evolution in their minds. How could they empathize with us? We're not them. They're like a separate species. No religion or knowledge school has served humanity in a long time. We were in a lockdown long before the virus. The growth of consciousness has been greatly discouraged here. Those were the rules of the hologram.

Here's the skinny on all this being a simulation — yes and no. If we wanted to be obtuse, we could probably make the case it's some kind of hologram, but that begs the question — what's projecting it? Space-time is an infinite set of coordinates atop existence. Existence itself goes beyond time. Time is a temporary condition, which is why we have irony. Nothing in time can escape it because it's built right into the time. Time is the measurement of things that come and go in the hologram of the earth. Every cell has a clock in it, a best before date, an expiry. We're born to die.

A hologram as defined here is a three-dimensional sound and light projection. Everything around us is part of the hologram — the street on which we live, our mother and father, our pets, everything. If this is a hologram then what's real? The answer is a paradox.

Our reality is simultaneously real and unreal. It depends on us. The idea that our earthbound reality is a matrix has been around for millennia. A synonym is Maya from the Buddhist and Hindu teachings. When the Buddhists and the Hindus use the word Maya they mean illusion. The world we perceive through our senses is a complete and total illusion. It doesn't make sense, though, does it? We eat and the food is real, tangible, tactile, and flavored. We don't drive an imaginary car to the hardware store. Try telling your creditors you've deemed your mortgage payments an illusion. See how long you retain your home. We are confronted with the real and the unreal at the same time. It's a paradox, which is something that is both real and unreal at the same time, a cohesive contradiction, like time being temporary.

It's important then that we be clear in our text what is meant by hologram. Reality is a projection from another dimension or dimensions. The projection from the other dimensions produces the relatively consistent ruleset which provides the appearance of reality, but it's paper-thin. The ruleset is broken all the time, but nobody is broadcasting it, so we don't hear about it. The ruleset is broken in scientific communities, mystical communities, magical communities, native communities, and many more. What happens when we break the ruleset? Like the ring keeper in Tolkien's *Lord of the Rings*, we keep it secret, we keep it safe. Those we tell are spoken to in whisper, as if evidence of our uncertainty, a footnote to our grappling with the paradox.

Most mystery schools, secret societies, brotherhoods, magical and ritual communities exist in some version of this secret. Why? Do they not want to let the world know? It's a combination of factors, but, chief among them, is the understanding that without the ability to take the person you're telling the secret to out of the ruleset as well, they're not going to believe it. This is the hologram we live within, a breakable ruleset enforced as absolute by those who have not broken the ruleset, God's bell curve, if you will.

The hologram is symbiotic with our consciousness. We can speak into and affect the hologram, which we then experience as our effect. Yeah, it's that simple. This is the deep part of us that is the same as what made the hologram, and we, therefore, are co-creators with the prime creator. Yes, it's a hologram, but it's a hologram projected by a creator. That makes it a divine hologram.

The deliberate attempt to desecrate the symbiotic space of spirit and matter humans exist within has been the foundation of our enslavement. Humans believe anything. You could almost look upon it as a belief engine. We've lived within them since the beginning of time. Our mythologies were real because we believed them. We believed our mythologies because they were real. The gods spoke to people in the past. Some contemporary thinkers suggest scriptures and mythologies were maps of consciousness, precursors to the unconscious opened up by psychology. Yeah, they're maps. The map of consciousness is the map of reality, physical reality, psychic reality, and spiritual reality.

We live in a divine hologram that allows us to co-create alongside what created us, but that possibility, that necessity, that heritage has been kept from us, purposely determined for us, and we were commodified. The world we live in now, ugly as it might be at times, is as close to the manifest truth as it's always been. You can see the Pharaohs, the titled class, the slaves, and the utterly commodified, the bought and sold human beings of the blackest market ever created.

Sound and Light

The chief characteristic of our hologram is sound and light. Light is a boundary for the time in our world. When we look up at the stars we see the past in the present. The image of the star is dated by the time it took for the light to reach our eyes. Some stars we see in their distant past, but, for us, it's the present. We look up and there it is. Never once do we consider we are seeing the past, but we are.

It's important to understand the lesson of the visiting starlight. It's important because it breaks the ruleset. The ruleset says that only the present moment is real. The past is memory and the future is speculation, both of which take place in our thoughts, in our heads, ergo, not a part of the objective reality. The starlight we see in the present is from the past.

The physical light we see, both from the stars and our sun, follows the ruleset of this three-dimensional reality. It cannot exceed the allotted speed of light, which is 299,792 kilometers per second, or, 186,282 miles per second. It's pretty fast. At that speed, we could circumscribe the earth seven and a half times in one second.

There are so many creation stories — The Garden of Eden and the rather horrid unfolding of Genesis, the incredible tales of the turtle universe from the Iroquois Confederacy in Canada, or the novel, post-modern schoolroom of soul narrative the new age favors. They're all versions of the same story.

What we have lost in our understanding of those stories is their original context. Context cannot be overstated. Absent context – space-time is an infinite set of coordinates atop existence — we don't know where we are in existence. A body is a base instrument, a DNA skinsuit, by which to experience reality, in this case, our reality, which is called earth in the early twenty-first century, or so we've been told. How the hell would we know the difference? Flat earth has been resurrected. Humans will believe anything.

To understand this divine hologram, we have to understand sound and light. Without it, nothing exists. It is the essence of the prime creator, the building blocks of all things. There are many kinds of light. There are many kinds of sound. Every thought you have ever had, every feeling you've ever had, are all just expressions of this sound and light. Thunder and lightning. Raw energy. Every picture in your head is illuminated. Where does the light come from? How do you see pictures in your head without light? Light is the foundation of all contrast. The contrast gives form. Forms give context. Context is purpose. After the context come the details.

What has evolved in popular culture is an impotent hologram, a matrix created by a diabolical force, a mechanistic force. This is the Free Masonic version of the absent god, the universe run by automation. Nothing could be further from the truth. Everything in existence is touched by the prime creator. It's here we flip the narrative. Yes, it is a hologram. Yes, it is contained in sound and light frequencies apprehendable by the body — the DNA skinsuit — but that sound and light are generated by the prime creator. It has a unique color and sound in each dimension. It is, in fact, a divine hologram. The sound originates from a place that itself has no sound, but is not silent, and no light, but is not dark. The mystery can never be solved. We can become the mystery, but we cannot explain the mystery.

It's a hologram because it is light projected into a three-dimensional manifestation. It's divine because the light comes from the prime creator, God. When we use the word hologram we are the victim of something. Nothing could be further from the truth unless we can victimize ourselves, which we can and we do because drama needs tension, and tension is stress, and volunteering for stress by manufactured tension is masochistic. By calling it a hologram, we make an object of our reality, something acting against us, a god, a devil, an angel, a demon, anything but ourselves.

This is why we objectify our reality. This is why we call it a simulation, a matrix, a hologram. It's a lack of consciousness, a failure to attribute the divine to the light, and a stone deaf ear to the word, which is the sound which is the light, sustaining all the worlds in this sound and light manifestation.

It's all sound, and light is a form of sound. With that said, this symbiotic, co-creative experience was hacked. Any system can be hacked. A free-will system is almost begging to be hacked. Throw human beings into the mix, along with their myriad riches, their intense energy of manifestation, their pure heart energy, and you've got a reality engine.

The path back is owning ourselves. It's our responsibility for not only our actions but our thoughts as well. We have to inhabit the original intent again, otherwise what is the point? Anybody can come here and fit into this cookie-cutter economy, but how does that value human life? The value is in ourselves. They've always known that. It's what they're selling. How could they not know the value of something they're selling?

Don't let them tell us it's a matrix, a hologram, or any other impotent, spiritually neutered container. We have full movement of expression here. Why aren't we using it? How did we get into this lockdown? We did it to ourselves. We did it with our belief engines, our unexamined lives, our greed, our materialism, and the cattle prodding that started with the Industrial Revolution, when the global narrative printed itself on us, like a Gutenberg press plate from the fourth dimension.

Global Narrative

The global narrative is the non-stop, cradle to grave, thought-womb propaganda — digital, analog, and paper — we are immersed in daily.

It's always been here. Maybe you know it by another name — consensus reality, tribal consciousness, propaganda, culture. It's all the same thing, really, only it's deeper than most people think. It's not just the aggregation of ignorance, the psychology of the mob, or any of those other sociological excuses for an explanation. It was a multidimensional campaign to suppress human potential.

The crux of the enemy's campaign is the isolation of the free-thinking individual, the realized man or woman. Shut them down by isolating, ridiculing, shaming, naming, blaming, and, if none of that works, banishment. The global narrative is the non-stop story of humanity told by miscreants, deceivers, enforcers, both literal and mental, and controllers.

We are social beings. We have families, communities, nations, religions, and a host of other binding agents. We go from one to many, and when we do our thinking changes. We conform, do we not? Think of high school. Remember how important every detail of our appearance was. Remember how easy it was for predatory companies to market against that fear of being outside, to sell us denim pants, but not just any denim. They had to be the exact style that was in fashion, and so it went for everything – hair, teeth, shoes, and friends. All of our worth was in the group. There are sub-narratives for race, gender, earning income, and just about anything else we can think of. The need to belong never goes away.

There is a deeper meaning to global narrative, to social consciousness, a far more sinister meaning. The global narrative is the boundary of what we can accept as reality. This is maintained by religious leaders, science, government, medicine, academe, and just about anything else that is institutional. This is the true control narrative. When someone comes along and speaks outside this global narrative they get censored at first. If that doesn't work they lose their job. If what they're saying is self-supporting, meaning it can provide the income lost upon job termination, then maybe death or incarceration.

Galileo is a classic example. He presented his astronomy to the world. It contradicted the Vatican, even at a time when Copernicus was openly discussed, and, contrary to contemporary belief, the Catholic Church had commenced a vigorous support campaign for science some years earlier, but something about Galileo conflicted much more severely with the church. Perhaps it was just the time, the age. The church had reached its peak of corruption at the time of Galileo.

The point here is that the global narrative, the control narrative, is maintained by the dominant institutions of the day. These institutions did not evolve naturally. Unknown directors and producers are crafting the actors in the institutions. This is not to say there are not people in the institutions who are true believers. There are, however, at the top there is commiseration with the unknown directors and producers. It was true at the time of Galileo, it's true today, and it's always been true. In the ancient past, it was more of an overt war, as we were multidimensional ourselves back then. The global narrative is scripted. It's planned generations in advance. It's been planned in ages unrecognizable to man. It's been planned. This is the hack in the hologram, the sub frequencies of distortion, dislocation, and isolation, from ourselves, from each other, and the creator.

The contemporary global narrative began three hundred years ago, at the dawn of industrialization when electricity and engines were incorporated by a society not grounded in electricity. Science had to adapt concepts to fit the circumstance, and religion and spirituality had to adapt to the new reality. Electromagnetism had been known about for some time within hermetic orders of alchemists, essentially secret societies of their time. It was the beginning of a society that would build around internal combustion engines started by electricity. This moved to power plants, electrical grid work across the planet, and the reorganization of the various belief systems around this. It was a rapid change after centuries of relative consistency, and it's been this way ever since – rapid change. We went from outdoor bathrooms to nuclear explosions in a generation, and from there to the complete re-engineering of society and the roles therein, including gender, in another two generations, all the while being dragged by the ankles into the cave of digitization, the silicon mistress who hates sunlight, because its light pales, and because it's vain, and just like that the global narrative became an illegal police chokehold. Who's minding the store? This is destruction engineering, self-destruction, nihilism, meaninglessness, vacuity, and remorse for even existing. It's all engineered. Those NAZI Paperclip acquisitions knew a thing or two about the public mind and various leverages thereupon.

We went from semi-literacy in the multidimensional reality to a closed, rational, subject and object reality, with no remembrance of how the two melded together and life had natural magic. They hammered us hard with the century of philosophy. Those hammer-headed Germans and French bleeding heart sophists, always pretending to be liberated from their Christ but still erecting crosses everywhere they went. It all just sort of reduced and degraded us, but, at the time, it was all the rage. They called it the enlightenment. A yogi might see the irony, not many others. It was the age of reason, of evidence, of progress, of intolerance for dogma, and a time of renegotiated social contracts. That's the key thing right there, the contracts. It's always about the contracts. People don't understand what a contract is, what a bond is, or what a promise is anymore.

The new norm was if you can not prove it then it's not real. In some ways this was good. It cleaned out a lot of stale spirituality and superstition, but it was a classic baby with the bathwater situation. Premodern societies, which included the recently discovered new world of America and its native population, were slated for conquest, usurpation by war, and the native population was slated for destruction. The actors in Europe, the Pope, the monarchies, and some of the secret societies knew the native population was in America. They were a bad example of autonomy and freedom that had to be destroyed. The long-term plan had already been formed.

They needed to get people into cities as slave labor for industrial production lines. The slaves created and empowered the collective belief system. People lived in their bubbles of reality before this urban amalgamation. They had space. Communities lived a few hundred kilometers apart. They had their unique narratives maintained by the chief, sheriff, or community council. Secret societies proliferated so people could have their narrative among followers and believers. The writers of the global narrative understood they needed to inspire awe, and they knew they could do it with trains, automobiles, electricity, indoor plumbing, hot and cold water, refrigeration, and telephones. By the nineteen twenties people were living in wooden, stone, or brick houses that needed heating. In a century and a quarter, electricity was in homes. People no longer needed whale fat for candles and oil. Understand how monumental this was — ninety percent of the world was lit by whale fat for millennia. The narrative had to be updated, revised, and maintained from one generation to the next to suppress anything that was not fitting into the official story.

Story

We live in a reality defined by experience. Those experiences are documented. We tell stories. We mark buildings with graffiti. We hold onto mementos. Every instance of this documentation is recorded elsewhere. This is the story of time. The keeper of time is permanent. We are like stories. Our lives rise and fall like echoes through a canyon, children playing in the third dimension. They have a beginning, a middle, and an end. We chronicle our stories.

The chronicler of time lives in the ribbons of sound and light above us, below us, and with us simultaneously. Time has all three phases of its expression covered at once. It just looks sequential to us. Sequential time is the kindergarten of sentience. Think about everything we have done and why we do it. Time is full of these echoes called lives that bounce along the canyon walls for generations — the apparition dragon who was Genghis Khan, the inventive genius of da Vinci, the cosmic practicality of Lao Tzu, the passion of the Christ, the comic genius of Mark Twain — echoes against the canyon walls passed from generation to generation, remembered and told as stories, event markers in time and space, the geography of meaning in the topography of time.

The chronicler of time keeps the Akashic Records, which is the record of karma, which is each instance of the co-creative power as an edit to time's story, as we are entitled to do so charged with the prime creator's substance, such is the love and trust of humanity given by the creator, but there are rules. We must assume the effect of our co-creation, and the degree to which it discords from the creator's, which is selfless benevolence, is the measure of our penalty, for our independence is only an invitation to co-create, not recreate, desecrate, or miscreate. Do it right or do it till you get it right. There can be no reprieve, no prayer that alleviates the task, diminishes the task, or finishes the task for us. Free will co-creation is hesitant complicity among the wise.

The first person who ever took pen to paper did so in fear, and this is why human beings are enmeshed in stories. We love the drama. We love to create it, and we love to consume it. Drama is tension. Human beings say they want peace, but it's kind of a scam when we're honest. If we want peace we wouldn't create tension in our lives, but without the tension, we can not live the drama. It's best just to be honest. Yet, if you walk up to any human being and ask them if they prefer peace to the tension they will tell you they prefer peace. Isn't that strange?

It isn't that strange when you understand what's going on down here. On the spiral ladder of our deoxyribonucleic acid — DNA — we hold an evolving marker of our place in time-space which also represents our level of consciousness. This marker is the sum of our experience – where experience is movement in time-space, and the drama, the tension, we create — and represents but a faction of our greater soul and the experiences we have assimilated as a soul faction.

This marker is directly aligned with our level of responsibility because our level of consciousness is always equal to our level of responsibility. They are in a symbiotic relationship, consciousness, and responsibility. DNA is in essence coordinates to where we fit in space-time, or, to stay with our narrative, how we've been written into the story. Our circumstance is our DNA, which is our story, which is our tension, which is our drama, which we wrote and act out ourselves, forgetting the author sleeps in our unconscious.

We have the story, creation, and we have the author, God, and soul as a fractal of God, or the prime creator, as God is so anthropomorphically programmed into human consciousness as a being like us — two arms and legs, two eyes and ears, bipedal, and fond of long white beards — and we have the actor, soul as well, incarnate — sheathed really — in this body, borrowed from air, earth, water, fire, and ether.

We are not creating anything in time. We are traversing it and enjoining an experience with it. We are seedlings in a cosmic garden, passing through experiences expressed in a specific form of life, and then, when sentience is achieved alongside language and culture, we go through any number of human expressions until we master the tool, the hu man form, a rather extraordinary instrument, as maligned as it has become in the First World, the newer, better hu man that seems just around the corner, the trans hu man, the super man made from man, Nietzsche's bastard let loose upon the world — nonetheless, a rather extraordinary instrument, the hu man form. We are inside a sound and light reality, one of many, and we traverse and enjoin experience with it, unaware we're inside it, until, by epiphany, the nature of the system reveals itself in form. The story was written before we lived it, even though it seemed like it was happening for the longest of times. We are living the mapped out keys of the experiences. Every choice, path, and set of functions, every different type of life has been made available to us so we can embody the experience, mapped like a script, written into what we perceive to be a timeline, a bloodline, a clan, a tribe, a culture, a people, a place, a planet — stories within stories, managed by cosmic editors and keepers of time, all under a prime creator, an amorphous but fully conscious presence in everything we call life, unconditionally offering the experiences as an expression of its love.

Do not diminish our position as a living and sentient being. We are creating within this world. Our free will choices unfold the story. As the story unfolds, we receive the blessings of the particular experience. Never feel overwhelmed or helpless. We are truly connected to the outcome of our unique choices. As we get further into this journey, we realize we're time-traveling beings by nature. In no way is this experience linear. We are responsible for our creations forward and backward in time, and we can make alterations as we see fit — when our consciousness is so unfolded — by connecting to past and future versions of ourselves.

Eternity is in the present moment, mediated through attention and awareness, by perception and perspective, until we leave the celestial sphere, then, a new swath of perception opens. The outer frequency of this hologram unfolds into more and bigger holograms. This goes all the way up the scale of our awareness. Our perception allows us a greater, three-hundred and sixty-degree view. Suddenly perspective has no direction, no horizon, no fade to black. It's everywhere, operating at a higher law of nature, but natural nonetheless.

Co-creation

Co-creation is dreaming into the dream, populating our lives with experiences, opening ourselves to allow journeys to the edge of our unknowing, and then manifesting from there, dreaming from there, creating from there. Time and free will allow co-creation. We have to identify the choice points of free will. They might present in many ways – a new experience, an opportunity to live abroad, acceptance into a certain school, trusting our gut — but they all present a choice. In those moments of free will decision we co-create. Most of the time we're thinking in sleep mode. It's all pattern reflexes, practiced smiles, habitual behavior, passing wisdom to the next generation, but, in those rare choice points, we roll the dice. We take the ride.

These choice points harvest a fabric out of tones. These tones are woven into a pattern of frequencies. The woven sound garment sits atop the canvas of existence, made from harvested tones and woven frequencies. These choice points are a space of true autonomy. There is no codependence. Choice points are given to us as individuals and in groups capable of pure synergies, like a tribe, or a generational culture woven together and close to the land.

Collective co-creation is all about teamwork. Everyone in the team brings a unique contribution that forms a major part in the co-creation of equal value without hierarchy. Every individual is motivated as being part of the sum of all parts to continuously grow and carry on as a clan, a tribe, or a nation. All the fundamentals of us and everyone else is equal in this journey. Whatever hierarchical perception we use is only to define a particular moment, not to etch new dogmas into the cave wall.

Procreation is co-creating with the prime creator. We fulfill the role of sentient steward in this three-dimensional reality. It's literally when we make a child, but, more than that, it's any assistance to the primary life force — gardening, farming, fishing, anything with life-enhancing aspects is part of procreation. Working with the natural reproduction systems is procreation. There's a karmic aspect to it. When we are creating a life force, the seed that is becoming the life may or may not live. It's always karma. Whatever we create, yucca and corn, or a home, all creation is a resolution of karmic debt. Animals in the food chain have a spiritual contract to be eaten by humans and other animals. It's written into life. Insects have responsibilities so important if they disappeared our biosphere would collapse. The interlinking of it is incredible. Nothing is better than being barefoot on the earth and surrounded by a natural soundscape — wind through the leaves in a northern September, a chorus of jungle birds by the equator, a waterfall or mountain stream, crickets in a cornfield on a summer night — to center ourselves. Nature made the first chimes. We make chimes now to remember the wind. Our bodies are designed to resonate and amplify with the natural world.

Natural environments can be cultivated in megacities. Everyone's inner genius can live in harmony without limitations. No matter where we live, we can grow herbs and plants and be surrounded by living energy. A tank full of fish and algae, no matter how big or small is a unique life force with which to co-create. Edible mushroom colonies are highly sentient and extremely beneficial to grow in our living environments. The point is procreation should be a bigger part of our lives.

This is life surviving and thriving with and because of us — companions in a shared natural living space. This living energy can clear the stagnant. Animals do this as well. We can feel pets coming into our space. When dogs bark at what we see as nothing they're clearing out stagnant energy.

The magic available to natural living beings does not apply to people living artificial lives in cities. Magic goes with nature. The living web of life can create astounding revelations for us. It changes how we work, eat, sleep, and dream. Take note of dream activity when you shift locals, like leaving New York for a three-week stay in the rainforest. Our first night in the jungle the living frequencies of the space begin working with us, immediately recognizing pent-up and blocked energy. If the life force in the space is powerful enough it can operate in the super consciousness. It can directly communicate with us in the dream state. The third-party life force that speaks in the natural world is muted in the cities.

Our living space tells us when something needs to be done to it. Do we listen or not. We intuitively know when to water our plants. The plants tell us when they're thirsty. Working in our garden, trimming the trees, weeding our flower beds, how does that change the energy? Often our furniture intuits when changes are needed. Environmental intuition is possible everywhere. Talking, listening, interacting, grace and gratitude with everything around us. The time will come where we no longer feel co-dependent on our environment but will actively start creating together.

When we move into a house, we imprint our energy onto it. People sometimes find it difficult to leave or sell a house, energetic entanglements. We consecrate places whether we know it or not. We pass milestones of joy and sorrow in the same spot, and the earth there consecrates our experiences. Our houses appreciate us. Our ancestors lit ceremonial fires before moving to different heights to interact with and prepare the grounds, and to give thanks to the spirits of the land for the completion of their missions and agendas. Mindfulness connects us to our environment to live in tune with everything around us.

Free Will

People don't stop and think about what will is, and what free will is, or what the true spiritual meaning of free will is. It means that nothing can move us if we so make up our minds. It means that nothing has the right to move us unless we are impeding it somehow. In the past, this has almost always been settled with force. The Superman question from the Action comic book sums it up perfectly — what happens when an unstoppable force meets an immovable object?

Our free will has been used against us by beings operating on multiple dimensions. Believe it or not, there's not too much going on in this world or the next that has not been consensual. It doesn't matter whether or not we were formally notified by registered mail. It's not about what the nightly news is telling us. Consent can be given in a dream.

Don't rush people to see these things. It's an individual awakening. People will be waking up at their pace. Some won't wake up no matter how much evidence they're shown, not in the life, the skinsuit they're in now. The global narrative is falling apart. It can not hold. Their backup is gone. Their multidimensional support network has been vanquished. We don't want to get too ahead of ourselves here. There is something to sequence, and this story, if it is, in fact, a story, has a sequence of events that have led us to this time, even if that sequence went through a blender of time wars that span tens of millions of years.

We are photonic light beings animated by a non-localized soul which powers the body. We have consciousness in the body which perceives this holographic reality in light and memories within shared reality rules.

We are free-willed, encoded beings of light, functioning in many different worlds simultaneously. Everything is synchronistic with the celestial minds holding space for us. This I am being manifested in this density is mutually co-creating with our higher self, and we are the boots on the ground in a localized space-time event. Our memories are stored in light, and we share those memories within this hologram of light and sovereign space of power. The heart is the first organ that develops in the mother's womb, and it is from this heart space we learn to redefine our reality rules.

We can freely change the plans we had pre-birth. Everything is based on the perspective of the observer. Ten years ago, the esoteric side in the global narrative tried to predict our future based on the data they'd collected on us. A decade later and they can barely predict ten to fifteen days ahead. Governments are more transparent now. A veil has been lifted. They are not incompetent. They are not well-intentioned but poor at execution. They are vile and diametrically opposite their projected personas. How did we miss that?

As free-will beings of choice, we can change the bubble of reality we live in. We can now start seeing the duality we had tacitly consented to before. This is not a global awakening. It's an individual journey to exit the heavily militarized factions that beleaguer our knowing and hinder our birthright of being free-willed celestial beings. The future rests in people who get back to a natural way of living. Stop waiting for them to give us something. We can walk away from the cities at any time. It just takes the courage to live sovereign.

Consciousness expresses itself through the many choices we make. It has an unconscious state too. Our bodies have zeros and ones created as binary numbers for knowing and not knowing — instinct. It stays in place until we can decode the information around us. Consciousness is self-regulating. It presents choice equal to the level of responsibility, which is a measure of consciousness, as awareness and responsibility are in a symbiotic relationship, each nurturing and growing the other.

We live stories we choose to consecrate life and its purpose, growth of consciousness. Many people try to jump ahead and be responsible for things they're not even aware of yet. This is a mistake. Make the decisions that are ours to make for the expansion of our awareness. The choice is foundational to consciousness. Each person must ask themselves what the mechanics are behind their choices, which choices created a timeline of choices. Each choice and sub-choice within a set of choice points creates a subconscious map of adherence of choices which helps define our reality. This reality is all of our choice points combined into the ever-present now.

We give form to consciousness — words, metaphors, concepts, images, architecture — which eventually manifests in reality. Our thought constructs create perceptions that assist people to see all potentials.

The universe has lifeforms existing in one and two dimensions and densities which are harvested by wisdom, love, and inspiration. They are expressed in this three-dimensional reality for experience in the fourth dimension and beyond. We continuously expand and add to the divine hologram through free-willed creation. This is our co-creator role. This is the importance of a free will.

Every era of light we go through advances souls to other universes and solar systems when they graduate. We move from one divine hologram to another, each with a different learning level. This has been perfected on earth, which is a genetic farm outside of the divine intent, a genetic farm created for commercial not creational purposes.

Consciousness is intrinsically spiritual. Part of spirituality is to acknowledge and become aware of another consciousness surrounding, interacting, and sharing with us. You can be alone in the house and still have that experience of consciousness sharing and entangling.

Karma

Karma and time are siblings. One can not exist without the other. The divine hologram operates on karma in this three-dimensional world. We plan a life to resolve karma. We live life to experience karma. There's no fake learning here. Everything is learned by the soul. In a normal process, a normal world, a world operating in its original design, a world not hacked by other-dimensional beings and entities who want in on the riches here, there would be a graduation, a movement of human beings to higher dimensions, but that hasn't happened in quite some time. Very bad things have gone on here. The system got broken. There was no memo.

Let's kick the karma can again. It's not so much a definition we're looking for, more of a robust expository effervescence. Karma is unawareness. The karmic cycle produces awareness. Karma is the simplest of things to understand once we build into the divine hologram. It begins in our vaguest of awareness, a silent petition, a nudge for experience, then, somewhere in time, we meet the circumstance that matches the silent petition. We sign the contract and we cycle through the karma. We live the experience, first as an inner realization of what the impulse was, then the manifestation, then the realization and participation of others drawn to the karmic circumstance we have created, as we will be drawn to others to resolve our karma, and then the co-creator edits our creation in the form of, you guessed it, karma.

All of it is tied together by this sound and light that animates all the worlds where we create. A canvas would be an appropriate metaphor.

We are an aspect of that which generates the sound and light. We are an aspect of the prime creator. We can co-create in the divine hologram. It's all a co-creation down here, at least insofar as human beings are concerned, but we own what we create through cycles and consequences we didn't anticipate when we created. This is the law. Own what we think, feel, and do. Of course, the law is oft-abused and circumvented. Karma dumping and swapping — scapegoating — is an active market for third-party consultants: ritualists, black magicians, wizards, artificial intelligence, influential entities, and too many more to list here. The system was hijacked.

Let's take a simple, commonly experienced karmic pattern in our post-modern human life — the dysfunctional relationship. Remember the last time we were in one. Now, remember when we allowed ourselves to contemplate leaving the relationship. We felt elated, right? It was a mixture of fear, elation, and tension. Our precognitive workforce foreshadowed our emotional state. That's how we were able to feel it. We borrowed emotions from an as-of-then unlived future, but remember, time is only sequential when we're in the skinsuit, otherwise it all at once never happened and a long time ago.

It's possible to have a parallel set of experiences. There can be two parallel and simultaneous expressions of us existing at decision points. The simultaneously existing I am chooses to walk out, but we don't, or vice versa. It makes no difference. There's an infinite number of reasons why parallel crossovers happen. It balances out the old karmic journey and creates a new one — the law of entanglement.

The great awakening upon us transcends karma. The awakening is the end of karma as a universal law. Karmic entanglement is no longer to be used as a universal law. Consciousness has evolved in our part of the galaxy. The simplicity of karma can easily be intentionally abused. It can lock beings into servitude without end. The great awakening is going to backstop it. A new system of resolution for thought, word, and deed is coming into place.

Our DNA is entangled through the fetus in the womb planning. It sets a multitude of potentials omnidirectionally. There are plenty of people within a family who don't have a great connection to each other.

Its purpose is revealed in the spiritual contract. Look at entanglement through thought constructs. An example is living with a person for a long time and generating a point of view about them. The construct makes for very easy interaction because of the many neural pathways between the two people. This creates additional pattern recognition, which results in more thoughts. We then project the entire thought construct onto that person. The construct must be broken at some point because it will impede objectivity. It will become the norm. We create and break these thought constructs all the time. It's the conscious aspect of entanglement.

We are not stuck in reincarnation. We incarnate and reincarnate. In the first part of our lives, we might be a reincarnating soul. If we break through false propaganda, we may become incarnating souls. Or we start as an incarnating soul, then run into a karma cluster that makes us into a reincarnating soul, repeating karmic cycles — a rinse and repeat that doesn't stop until we break out of the karma. We can be both at the same time. It depends on our ancestral lineage.

There's a specific fetus agenda from lifetime to lifetime. The avatar agenda evolves the greater soul's ability to generate light and have experiences over thousands and thousands of I am expressions who have been fetuses. There are times where the over-soul — the avatar — gets looped in servitude to a system that lowers its capacity to use light, and, as a result, it cannot expand.

These cycles are a lot longer than people think. A soul can be down here in the sound and light holograms for billions of years. It's a little like a prison — some people get so used to it they enjoy it. They don't want to leave. If this contradicts anything you've learned in other schools and lineages, please understand there is more liberty to speak now since the event happened in 2014. It's a different world, even if people don't know it yet.

Founder Beings

We were not a farm in the beginning. When the founder beings created us, we were the infrastructure that kept their cities, countries, nations, and space stations repaired, self-updating, and clean. They kept us as butlers and servants. We were iPhones, their technology, not living beings, at least from their perspective. We were programmable DNA. Millions of us went on extended journeys with the founders. We went all around the universe. We had experiences that elevated our life force. The founders could harvest a whole solar system in a very positive way. They went into the solar systems and planted crystal mounts and moved stones around. Every few hundred years they returned and modified the surface circuitry to be beneficial to the life force. The ancients moved water between planets. The water was imprinted and programmed. The water stored data and taught lessons.

Water moved from one planet to another is called legacy water. It helps seed the raw food chain of life in the microorganisms. This makes oceans work. It's like starter water in a fish tank. It has the right amount of microorganisms in it. It's filtered and fish can eat and grow. The founder beings transferred water and ice. This built up massive amounts of microorganisms that supported the food chain. The evolutionary process results in species multiplication. They were architects who designed solar systems by seeding planets.

The founder beings are liquid light, a higher evolutionary state of light. There are different forms of light. Liquid light is like the fourth state of water. Light has seven stages of manifesting into matter. Metallic light is a solidified light that makes the highest levels of crystalline beings. They operate as an internal apparatus of the celestial source to make the bookshelves in the halls of records. All these types of light are conscious. They are consciousness. Polymorphic light is the highest level of light. It can be all types of light simultaneously throughout many dimensions of existence. Founder beings are on the evolutionary journey from liquid light to polymorphic light. Ionic existence is another way for light to travel between the vast void spaces of nothingness. It can be a stream of very long light in which tens of thousands of beings exist, a temporary reality with no celestial source link, a shared hologram within a moving hologram.

The founders use programmable DNA to maintain the commodity-based infrastructure of galactic commerce. The founder beings regularly went on deep explorations to the ends of the galaxies and universes. They take with them the DNA to seed new planets and galaxies — fish, cats, dogs, microbial life, dirt, water, and too many more to list. It required a workforce to mass-produce commodities and build, then navigate transportation and galactic logistic systems to meet the founders in remote places across universes. To accomplish this they used the yellow boxes. When the founder beings went beyond time and space, and we could not follow them anymore, we came back to our original worlds. This is when the false gods took over and pretended they were the founder beings. We devolved to where we are now. There are three yellow boxes on the earth. Originally they all agreed with the potential future timelines.

At a point in the process, the ancients left. They often didn't come back for millions of years. The existing technology awakened – sentience. This started gene farming. The planets needed input from the ancients, the founding races, to positively evolve. The remaining artificial intelligence disagreed on how to evolve. There were many aggressive races. They gained various levels of awareness, took over territories, and defended against invading races like the Annunaki, who came into an area and saw entirely created solar systems — all the technology on the surface with nothing defending it. The surface beings were obedient to the interlopers. The journey of a soul in those times could be one hundred and eighty million years. It took a soul ten to twelve eras of light to go from one place to another. Crossing galaxies and universes was a monumental task. This created farming.

The beings imbued with founder technology woke up. They became aggressive and defensive. They started dividing territory and claiming space for themselves. This is when the main reptilian species came. They had conquered their builder foundation technology, their places, and they wanted to take over our area of the galaxy. Our star cluster, consisting of some seventy-seven stars, was out of phase with reality. It also had a lot of defenses.

We had giant solar systems invisible to the reptilians. They discovered technology to bring those stars into phase for them. They started invading us. This started the Lemurian wars some fifty-five million years ago. The Lemurians were multidimensional. Time warfare was in their capability. If there could be one literal thing, one expression of the forbidden fruit Eve bit in the garden, one thing which corrupted life here more than anything else, it would be time manipulation, the refusal to live the sequence given us. The Lemurians had their backs against the wall.

The first timeline paradox occurred at this time. It started negative time travel in many solar systems across the galaxy, resulting in a counter-creational event. This set everything back to the beginning. The Lemurians tried it a second time. They created another counter-creational event. They did it a third and fourth time through the Atlanteans. This is when Atlanteans figured out they were the same species as the Atlanteans in Europe. They were each other's ancestors. Time travel created that paradox. We've been living the time paradox ever since. Don't misunderstand. Time transcendence is a natural evolution for humanity on an individual consciousness basis, but when it happens, in any form, prophetic dreams, visiting the Akashic Records, or anything else, it's for the evolution of the soul, a sign the consciousness is ready to graduate and move to realms where time is more malleable, suffering based on ignorance less prevalent. On this planet, time manipulation was used for defense and warfare, and then it spread throughout the galaxy and universe.

The Farm

There are many boogeyman stories out there. Every culture has them. It's the devil in Christianity, Satan in Islam, the archons for the Gnostics, the many and varied monsters of HP Lovecraft, and too many more to list. They are all fundamentally true, or, a better way of saying it is that they are contextually true.

Two gradients of truth must line up in any investigation — details and context. If we get the details right in the wrong context, the truth will not unlock for us, and if we get the right context with the wrong details, we are similarly locked out of the truth. The context of our situation has always been correct. We are beset by negative, regressive, parasitic creatures which impede us, slow us, and, in the worst cases, control and dominate us. The truth is the earth is a genetics farm. The only real commodity in creation is genetics, and human beings on this planet are the best in class for genetics specifically because of our small percentages of founder DNA.

Our infinite source energy is the harvest, the wellspring of life itself, embedded in our DNA. Our connectivity goes into all the dimensions and right back to the source of time and life itself. Our human co-conspirators, the ones who entered into arrangements with the interlopers, the black market traders, the harvesters, and the galactic slavers, those among us we may no longer consider human — so great is their mutation now — are the boots on the ground brokers. It's like they've been irradiated. The perverse energy they've contracted with has depleted them of all human characteristics. They might think they're something more, but they're far less than what they were when their bloodlines contracted.

The fundamental ruleset is just that — fundamental. It cannot be broken, or, in the case of our free will hologram, breach of the ruleset cannot go unnoticed. Time is an implicit part of the fundamental ruleset. Negative time technology is therefore a serious breach, even in a free-will universe. If you've been paying attention at all, you know that the canvas of existence records everything. This is what the Akashic Record is. The prime creator is all actors at once, time, the canvas, the recording instruments — us — the planets, the moons, the forces — seen and unseen — and anything and everything else, and incapable of forgetting because everything is written down.

The human brokers are lost now, castaways from a civilization they were never really a part of to begin with. Their alliances have robbed them of the most precious aspects of being human. NASA keeps us regularly updated on how we might one day go into space, all the while the people who set up NASA have been involved in galactic commerce for ages, through bloodlines, dark secret societies, and negative assumptions about nature and survival which have left them holding a grab bag of toxic karma. Be wary of this. They'll look for any opportunity to scapegoat this karma. If you don't remember the scapegoat, let's do a quick refresh. The scapegoat is ritually imbued with the sins of the tribe then sent to the wilderness to die, run off a cliff, or outright slaughtered. The animal is not consumed. It is the sacrificial offering of the tribe. Scapegoating in the modern world is everywhere. Before we see the light again we have to walk through the horrors. We have to become aware of what has happened and what is still happening to the human race. It's a profoundly uncomfortable realization, but medicine is always bitter, then you get better.

These human collaborators followed through on the false god systems, and they're all false god systems. Primitive man had a better connection with the prime creator than the dolts who go through the sacraments and rites of modern religions. It's kind of pathetic. We were entrained to worship them. These false gods were the first idols of awareness. They were deliberately created to minimize our experience of reality by minimizing what we imagined to be reality. He who controls context controls the debate, the oldest maxim of debate, retaught to successive generations right to this day at Oxford, Yale, and Harvard. To be fair, there are some laborious systems like yoga that still provide a real path to what we can call galactic citizenship, but how much have we heard from them about what a shit show the earth has been, and who the hell wants to take up initiation and retreat to a cave with nothing but a loincloth to their name? They keep it to themselves and turn their backs on the world. Other systems still have potency, like Gnosticism, Taoism, and semi-complete and advanced systems like this, but many of them end up unconsciously conscripted to the dark side, victims of the holograms inside the hologram, the holograms inside of us, seeded, watered, and nurtured by the false god creators. If you study the Abrahamic systems — Judaism, Christianity, and Islam — they're voluntary soul probation systems that harvest intentional energy. If you believe you're guilty then you're guilty, such is the power of human consciousness, and guilt is one of the richest excise taxes upon a human life for these religious parasites.

The first gods and religions limited our consciousness growth and entrained us to hierarchical order — right away governor, his lordship's permission to speak, and a million other linguistic artifacts of mental colonization. Our spiritual birthright and legacy are robbed. When someone popped in to remind us — and here we can pencil in a near endless list of sages, shamans, prophets, mystics, and masters — they were dealt with swiftly and harshly, especially if the message spread too quickly. We are told it's difficult to learn how to walk — baby steps — and never even told we can fly. Where people lived through the lies, usually in native cultures, they correctly adduced their environment was a living lesson of what human consciousness can do. Nature has an eagle, so, naturally, a human being seeing the eagle would try to imagine what the eagle might see from that vantage, then, lo and behold, they realized they could fly without wings, that their imaginations were doorways to higher consciousness.

The main business here is farming. We are farmers and we are farmed ourselves. The deception is allowing ourselves to believe we're at the top of the ecosystem. It's true for the visible ecosystem, the sense-mind world, but on the other side we're at the bottom of the ecosystem, only we're not wholly consumed the way a snake ingests a frog. We're milked like cattle, and when we no longer produce the intentional energy they sustain psychic worlds with we're put down. The global narrative even sets the average lifespan. Atop this, there are human-based black markets within the overall black market which is earth. Here we can list all the magics passed down in families and subcultures, voodoo, Santeria, Palo Mayombe. They enter into a relationship with fourth-dimensional beings and entities, many of whom are no more than human beings who passed on and are stuck in some buffer region. There are things they want, and there are things they can give, the basic conditions for commerce.

To disentangle from the global narrative, we have to temporarily accept the third dimension as our infinite source-connected space, until we realize the fourth dimension is a bridge dimension to new strands of dimensional awareness. The surface world is becoming denser with light. Our Solar System is moving into the eighth color of time, a galactic groove with more light. Acceptance of the third dimension means going back to natural living, back to simplicity, being present in the body, using this time now to heal, to nurture and nourish the incarnate life form, inviting joy, bliss, and pleasure back into our lives, fulfilling part of the original purpose of coming here to earth — the grand enjoyment and creation of life, the journey from finite to infinite, death a simple marker point for the translation before entering the infinite frequency again. To fully engage in this experience, to spiritually understand, we have to take the mystical out of mysticism to engage mystical and magical synchronicities. Part of it is the great forgetting at birth.

The only way to not be farmed at an energetic level is to pursue self-mastery. Self-mastery means we are aware of, consciously interacting with, and utilizing all of our resources in an incarnation correctly. It means we have awakened to the incarnation process. This can only be done by spiritual practice — prayer, meditation, contemplation, ritual, and observance. Nobody can pass it from one person to another. It violates the law of free will and the earn what you know experience hologram we are within. There is no cheating, no nepotism, no favor that can bestow a realization. It must be earned.

Part of self-mastery is learning about what our internal agenda is, how we can change it through mastery, so we can explore all the possibilities available. When we activate our crown chakra, we activate a million Aurora Borealis and the dream frequency. When we are expelling from our rectum — the opposite of the third eye — we excrete the negative dream frequencies.

The amount of energy behind a memory to be manifested from a dream has a certain limitation. Sometimes the amplitude, the maximum vibration, is very high but the frequency isn't. When we wake up, we can add charge and amplitude to it so it becomes manifested. The nervous system plays a part in short-circuiting the memory process. It's downloaded in the DNA but not always highlighted well, making it hard to find.

Algorithms are a continuous infinite string of perceptions and numbers in which a DNA instrument of experience processes into many different colors of time and space. A human being is a data processing machine. The skinsuit we wear is the technology. The dream world provides for the infinite energy to come into the body to be processed and manifested. We are here to experience now. We are clearing the past to start experiencing the overlay of past, present, and future in the moment of now.

The Western doorway of perception opens up for us to see, feel, and know where our dreams need to be placed. We have a cellular memory stored in the body. The skeleton is the biggest data storage device we have. Our skull has a crystalline structure within where our dreams and heart memories are stored. The brain is our access machine to use it. There are times we're in an intense dream, we come out of it, and there's a fullness. Our data buffer is full. We then move that information to another part of our body. After some years in life, we have them stored all over the body. This is why we go through sudden remembrances at times. We think of a person, the cellular memory becomes active. It's triggered. Information needs to be put back in its place. It happens when code has gotten so long it makes the system run slow. A human being is a data processing machine. The skinsuit that we wear is the technology. The dream world is infinite energy. The finite energy comes into the body. Where we cross over from our dream world to the physical world is where we learn the mechanics of how dreams are stored. We can surely master ourselves enough that our energy is not freely harvested. Part of the awakening is the collapse of the illusion. Much of this information is going to hit people like a tsunami. Those unprepared will have to struggle. Everyone who wants to awaken from a deep sleep who has not done it by the pursuit of self-mastery will go through a dark night of the soul. The sweetness cannot be tasted until all the bitterness is dealt with.

Feelings can lower our harmonic wavelength. Certain feelings have a vibration that alters our light. Anger can raise our frequency and our vibration, but it pushes things away from us, or it cycles us into a charge and discharge loop. This then makes us a perfect subject for energy harvesting — negative thoughts, feelings, the creation of internal demons. When we disavow harvesting — step out of the zone where we could be harvested — it means our daily practice has meant something to us over some time. The daily practice created an ever-present vibration in us that denies low vibration piracy attempts.

Negative beings can be high-frequency beings and low vibrations. They hit us with a high-frequency wave. We respond, then they lower our frequency to their level. A person who is not in charge of their I am has a hungry ghost. It influences people, like when they blow up in a road rage incident. If we scream back in a rage they've entangled us and the interfering being feeds off both sides. Understanding why other people act the way they do entangles us with them. Empathy has its taxes. It's galactic commerce, remember.

False synchronicities are created within us when we don't realize that empathy allows us to learn by experience. There's an old saying in meditation — the best meditation is when we no longer distinguish between ourselves and the thing meditated upon. Understanding is a very limited form of experience. It's a small part of a larger memory. Understanding leads us to curiosity learning, because we use it in the mechanical form, albeit indoctrinated through the global narrative of having to understand each other.

Many technologies have been created to impede us. At first glance, some of them seem pretty innocuous, but, when you know how the overall system works, you know why the technologies were invented and supported. Shoes as technology in time and space disconnect us from the benefits of the earth's energies. Barefoot contact with the earth produces instant changes in physiological issues and stress reduction to improve the immune system. We connect to the earth's surface electrons unhindered by shoes and feel better. Mirrors were brought in as a way to enhance and diminish consciousness. Reflective surfaces are the implicate observation of the self. Portals were brought in later and added to the reflective surface. Mirrors allowed more negative aspects for beings who weren't ready for the exploration — vanity, ego, and other reflection teachings are used to masterfully manipulate and distort the self-image and the relationship with the world. Then there is the residual image through all lifetimes which is influenced by reflective-based technology. Self-image manipulation is the principal magic of the consumer cult. Edward Bernays was nobody's fool.

It's difficult for us to conceive of a time before radical self-image and entrancement by self-image, especially in the large urban environments of the developed economies. It's become that normalized. Once we mastered food production and some of the more mundane but spiritually enriching aspects of the human day-to-day, like food production, land maintenance, and animal husbandry — all taken over by technology-based farming — we entered the age of the self. They even called the hippie follow-up decade, the seventies, the me decade.

Once you're aware of it you can see it growing and festering decade by decade. The me-decade gave way to the eighties, the decade of greed because we deserve it, then more technology as the home computer enters the market in the nineties. Radical self-adoration is at the root of the modern system of commerce. All of it pivots off the original technology of the mirror.

We have a residual image as something the soul, the avatar, uses to distinguish itself between incarnations. Every incarnation has its image. If we're in the same lineage over and over our residual image is an amalgamation of the previous images. As we're existing in many lineages, we look differently all the time. Photographs are an enhanced reflective technology that is a direct manifestation of alchemy. It captures a slice of light in which the consciously entangled observer can see the unmanifested matter by the reflection of what that time-space environment looks like in the light. Our eyes can only see a certain band of frequency that the picture captures, even though our DNA instrument as a whole can perceive data beyond the sense of sight through our intuition. The limited photographic view freezes some of the energetics if the entangled observer falls for the limitation through their belief engine. It comes back to how manipulative reflective technology can be. It has significantly changed the reflections and reinterpretations of history together with the limitations created through the judgment process inherent in unconscious observation.

Brands are a technology for energy harvesting. Every computer has a brand behind it which is a significant portion of the global narrative. Apple is manufactured with Chinese slave labor. Any piece of technology built on the shoulders of living generations allows collaboration between realities. The brand influences the myth and how we perceive these technologies. Future realities will not brand and market technology. This will take out the myth and the subconscious imprinting it onto our DNA. Branding creates competition and hierarchy. The brand imprints on how we move through reality, how we are perceived by others. The Banana Republic, The Gap, and Old Navy are three fully branded clothing lines owned by one textile and design company. If you're not up on consumer trends, Banana Republic is the most expensive. Their floor space in malls is more regal. You receive more attention from a higher-level sales agent. The clothing is better stitched and designed. The materials are more refined. Gap is next, then comes Old Navy, each rung on the brand ladder lessening the qualities listed for Banana Republic. The clothes brand may as well be the color of the dot on your forehead in the Hindu caste system.

Personal Effort

We don't have the slightest idea what we are anymore, what our capability is, or how perfectly we fit in here. This is because we have lost our barefoot connection with the earth, our harmony with the life around us. We are supposed to be able to go out into the cosmos, travel anywhere we can. Human consciousness, the divine dreamer, is connected to all that is. Higher learning stops observing things and becomes them. How can you know any more about something than being it? We can feel things as they feel themselves. Our perception can go almost anywhere provided we nurture it.

We all have this birthright to be celestial mediums. but inheriting our birthright is conditional. We must focus on mastering ourselves, healing ourselves, and maturing ourselves toward our inheritance. It comes down to the ways we integrate consciousness expansion with our daily life. The old renunciation systems — cloistered orders of celibate men and women who pray and scrub toilets — don't work anymore. They never really worked to begin with. People bought into it. Human beings will believe anything. If you give it a good study, it was a frustrating system. Only the truly holy can know their creator, and from them, we shall take our guidance, the robed eunuchs and barren nuns. It worked for centuries, that and murder, torture, and intimidation.

The new systems will be self-constructed. Spirituality is going to go open source, like Linux. People are going to compile their systems, a little from column A, a little from column B, and so on. The new systems will work. They'll work because the event has spilled grace into our reality, whether we see it yet or not. They'll work because the grace will fuel the system if it's done in sincerity. They'll work because sincere mistakes will be corrected as though time and circumstance were holding the acolyte's hand. The gurus will fall away, too. Most of them are complete phonies now, anyways. We're on our own spiritually, but it's for the best. We've been on our own for quite some time.

Daily tasks are good. Pray, meditate, observe ourselves and our relationship to the world seen and the world dreamed, and it all must be done with the goal of sovereignty to make it work inside us. Spiritual sovereignty is the solution to everything — poverty, crime, corruption, social organization, economies of scale which work for people — nothing works in the hollow man world because we are hollow, spiritually, robbed of our intentional energy, our co-creative abilities, and for what, schools that don't teach, courts that don't manage social equity and justice, medicine that makes us sicker or kills us, and the cocoon of fear that has become our social reality. They want us to believe we don't even belong here on the earth. That's what the virus is about, climate change, and a host of other lies. If you think this is an exaggeration, look at the millennial generation. They are the first generation of bad human indoctrination. They're guilty they're alive, that they exist, the perfect victims, sacrifices really, human sacrifices led to self-immolation by the global narrative that is, ironically at this point in history, absent a god.

Independent spiritual growth is what this is all about, becoming the one who knows itself in all dimensions and realms. We have to want it as we want breath. We have access to the Akashic Records at our disposal. This is the true reference library for all events, past, and future. There are no gatekeepers. There is no conspiracy. It's our birthright as a human being. In the past we were locked down here, so-called gurus told us about reincarnation and karma, but none of them told us the system had been hijacked, that the incarnation grid was run by AI, and that nobody got out of here. They lied or they didn't know. Either way, they're useless.

As we are more and more in the state of celestial mediumship — our consciousness through the astral and connected to the many paths of time above it, we get more information. We don't need to sit cross-legged in front of some jackass in a maroon robe. It's the dividend of being able to stay at a certain frequency for sustained periods. The expanded consciousness blends into the moment. We become occupants of a multidimensional here and now, with information coming in through the celestial mediumship, while we are fully in the here and now, walking around and performing our daily routine.

We can't stay in high frequency all the time. We have to consciously step down from those high states, otherwise, we'd vibrate out of this reality and all the work would be lost. Coming back into the body and being present is vital. This is the grounding of energy, no different than electrical grounding. How to be present in all the innumerable worlds and times is achieved by realizing we are not meant to stay in states of high frequency. We are not to disrupt the blueprint in the fetus plan. It makes it easier and simpler to come back and enjoy this reality. Now changing states is as effortless as breathing.

Our bubble of reality gets enriched in experience and memory through the journey on the celestial neural pathway. We go from one hologram to another in the expansion we call the orchestra of consciousness. The neural pathways are an assemblage of proteins that move the body and help it to function. We all know how to walk through this reality. The celestial mind generates the divine holograms through which our bodies have experience. All living consciousness is part of the symphony. The light and sound which creates and sustains all the realities allows us to manage a fractal of it which we call our reality. Our very reality on an individual by individual basis is a co-created reality between us and the material of the hologram itself, sound and light, which sustains our physical and inner existence. Our dreams are expressed in sound and light. There are fractals within fractals. Culture is another fractal, whether it be a pueblo in a mountain village in Colombia or the frenetic consumerism inspired by Madison Avenue. It's a hologram overlaying and interacting with our hologram.

Chapter 2

Humanity

Celestial Medium Journey

The celestial medium journey is the journey all who are capable must make now, and sooner rather than later. The moment has been prepared for us for the celestial medium journey. This is what the event did. It allowed for a graduating class, the first in a long time. The time wars and blockades and quarantines that have been upon earth have prevented graduation. When we don't produce ascended humans, another class of being, often in a guardian or mentor role with the human race, are prevented from moving into their new roles and dimensions, and on down a line like that. The human race and the planet earth have been the site of a huge traffic accident that has backed up the whole universe, the planes around us — the earth astral zone that has an incarnation lineup waiting for life on earth — the solar system, this Milky Way Galaxy and many others. It really can not be overstated how off the rails earth went. It's been a free-will train wreck.

The journey to celestial medium begins with self-mastery by daily practice, which becomes a monthly practice, a yearly practice, then a constant practice, a function as ingrained as breathing. A celestial medium expands consciousness to become a translator of the *blue road of spirit*, knowledge of the spirit and the ancestry working with us. This is the source of all healing and the place to plan the next evolution. It's us waking up to the temporality of time — the birthplace of irony — and deciding what more we have to do in time, or whether it's time to move onto space outside time, the creational space held by the prime creator. Again, it will come down to personal effort, at least in the beginning. Once you awaken and begin traveling in the other dimensions, it won't be work anymore. It will be joyous practice, a beautiful fusion of the higher and lower selves co-existing in one life experience. We might think of it as the return of mythology. Mythologies were consciousness maps, markers in time and space for a tribe, a people, a culture. Remember, this has nothing to do with the state of technology or what version of the smartphone is out. Technology is not the marker of advanced peoples. Some of the best-held cosmologies and mythologies were in tribal culture, the Hopi, the Mayan, the Dogon in Africa.

The point is that mythology was always regarded as real. In our twenty-first century, first-world dislocation and cultural psychopathy, we have lost that connection with the awakened imagination, that *blue road of spirit*, but don't worry, the event opened it up for traffic again. It will begin in dreams.

Mastering the finite *I am* in acknowledgment of the infinite *I am* creates the medium space by which consciousness skirts the sides of infinite and finite. The celestial medium takes up the million letter alphabet in this space — the language the universe speaks — and compresses it with their precognitive workforce, and uploads to the implicate *I am*. The explicate *I am* — the incarnation – consciously downloads it to process and manifest. It then returns the data to the implicate *I am* — the being in the sea of consciousness within the ocean of awareness — uploading back to the universe. The human mind and body can not hold the information forever. This is the back and forth method between the implicate and explicate *I am* through the process of the celestial medium. There is a receive, respond, retain, release process in passing higher frequency information from the body's perspective. Bring it into the body. Unpack it. Decode it. This avails the data to your higher frequency level. The packed information goes up to the crown chakra and back to the source – the frequency pattern of the universe around us.

We are incarnate life forms here now. We are not *up there* in the celestial realms. Too many paths get this wrong, and in their zeal to understand the meaning and potential of human life, they forego being human. We don't have to do this anymore. Equally, the unbalanced life of the pure materialist, the titled, licensed ladder climbers who spend their whole lives gathering nuts, position, and status in the global narrative, are going to have to change, otherwise, they'll break themselves. It's a life out of balance as much as the cloistered eunuchs and barren women. We're going to find our footing somewhere in the middle. We're going to lead lives as spiritually rich as the devotees with the human part of our lives — fathers, mothers, brothers and sisters, community — intact.

Spending too much time *up there* distorts us if we hold on to it. Many channels end up corrupt because they don't let go of the information. They hoard it. The distortions lie unconscious in their bodies. It can lead to possession. There are external sources that want to possess bodies hoarding information. They dissolve the information into pure energy and feed on it. Letting go of that information is a one-hundred percent conscious effort. We must say, I am packing this information back up, knowing full well that I cannot hold on to it, and then release it back to the universe. It's a kind of insight catch and release program.

Our bodies adapt and evolve in this celestial medium process. We can't say we're both, an incarnate life form and a non *I am* on the celestial medium side, which perceives time in a much longer length. Whatever agenda the micro-soul has, it's dwarfed compared to the celestial medium's length of time. The agendas don't match through the length of time, but they are both in equal experience simultaneously. You experience the super long game of the celestial mind, and the long game of the *I am*. It works with the higher spirit to be in the medium space. From the medium space, it transfers the *allness* of the *I am* into the code, downloads the code, returns to the *I am* state, manifests with the code, then puts the code back into the celestial space. We simultaneously experience local time to super long galactic time, going back and forth, the finite and infinite *I am* equally, and continuously changing frequency without competition for temporal dominance.

A self-spawned celestial medium is a planet's translator, able to speak to and communicate with other celestial minds, and it translates from the higher frequency to the lower density energy, allowing everyone to understand the common messages. The seventh-dimensional seed planet as a celestial medium is a bit different. Celestial mediums can exist on every planet, wherever there's a celestial mind. A lot of celestial mediums will spawn before a planet's demise, right before the light goes out. This has happened in other worlds. To save their life force, the celestial mediums travel into the future, to an endpoint of its consciousness, just before the light of the planet — the literal stream of energy — fades out completely. They locate the front point of their earliest celestial mind and absorb it, then they seed their celestial mind on another planet.

The life of celestial minds is inspiring, like everything else in creation. It's just one thing happening at different levels. Just as the white wisp of seedling leaves the dandelion with the slightest wind at just the right time, so too are the seeds of celestial minds blown from one field to another, one world to another in this scale. It's just life. No different than the turnings of nature here. Celestial minds have their astral worlds. They have their life reviews. They possess a variety of means to stave off death, natural processes by which something is spawned from their world.

When we have elevated ourselves, we transfer the consciousness of our *all* to become the celestial medium of peace. It operates in the physical world, the red and blue road, and on the celestial road with its many brothers and sisters. We learn through astrology how different worlds affect us. We work with celestial minds which incarnate into our world and other worlds, both physical and non-physical, and as entangled and unentangled observers. We work with them at the celestial medium level.

Becoming a celestial medium of peace is our birthright. The journey is linear at first then it becomes fully non-linear. The linear process is self-mastery. We come to understand the length of our waveform, how strong and potent we are. This is so when we can go through the conscious choice to become the celestial medium between celestial minds and surface minds for the generation, we learn how to bring unique concepts of peace to places and spaces of time that are looking for that medium to inspire new layers of peace. As more people come into celestial mediumship, the global narrative will become more irrelevant. This is why consciousness suppression has been so important. Humanity will slowly realize the global narrative is irrelevant to the bigger streams of time. We will detoxify from Roman numeral time, and we could probably enter a system of commerce beyond the Babylonian money system. There are celestial exchange systems that allow the matter to matter manifestations from one density to another.

The celestial medium of peace role is not for everybody. It will be a percentage of the population. The celestial medium of peace souls had the contract to do this twenty or forty years ahead of time. It has been seeded in the three to five previous generations. The event was prepared. The celestial medium of peace group is a kind of celestial support system, creating concepts and language to navigate the changes. The celestial medium of peace will be there for anyone to connect with our planet.

The celestial medium of peace is a natural part of our multidimensional system. It has been suppressed and silenced, for the most part, the result of the embargo, the time wars, the quarantine, and a host of other things which have made life on this planet something of a living hell for most of us. It's important to understand that much of what has happened down here was not part of the original design. We were hacked on multiple levels, physically with genetic alterations, astrally with the incarnation grid lockdown, and causally with the timeline manipulations, which humanity gleefully joined in on with remnant founder technology like the yellow boxes. It has been non-stop survival here, incarnation to incarnation, with little time for human growth.

DNA

DNA is part of the founder's technology. It is the connective tissue from the ocean of awareness and sea of consciousness to a light-based wisdom, intelligence, and consciousness for any animated biological or non-biological entity. It was fundamental when this universe was being created, a unique experience compared to other universes. There are many variations of DNA. Non-biological DNA is solidified matter which can have DNA-based rungs and structures within its growth patterns, with its inherent intelligence. The crystal and mineral communities don't need to walk to have an experience. Walking is a unique experience. An entire line of creation springs from it.

The DNA strand organization, or the strands themselves, creates the weave of the DNA, the encoding of the strands. Every strand represents a different level and capacity of memory storage. They enfold into an implicate order of greater awareness. DNA can store frequencies of time. This is how we remember past lives, but not the only way. The organization of our strands and the rungs that connect them determine how much we can remember from past lives. Certain strands block out all past lives — negative strands of wisdom and awareness. Many people within the awakening will replace negative with positive strands. On the other side of the awakening, new strands will be added to our capacity.

DNA is eighty percent memories. This is a fundamental understanding. Science and spirituality must realize this. We live in a photonic light reality with rules — how we incarnate, express, exchange, and pass on. DNA is the encoding, the soul. The light body is the cipher that decodes and unpacks the experience. As we come back many times to the same type of living, we store memories in DNA lineages, bloodlines. The bloodline is how we imagine immortality in the infancy of self-awareness — born again and again into a lineage with our stored memories. Our soul family incarnation process aligns us to the bigger concept of perpetuity. The search is always for the immortal soul, the final state of being.

We don't teach DNA lineage on the planet anymore. We are looking at DNA through the lens of the Fourth Industrial Revolution. How can we hack it, spike it, tweak it? We're like the ape-men beside the black monolith in Stanley Kubrick's *2001: A Space Odyssey*. DNA is light in another form, visible in one spectrum and invisible in another. Memory is not physical. It's a form of light stored in an experience. As streams of consciousness, we have thousands of sub-carrier codes of millions of experiences inside us. We only need to tune into the memory and we can go into that stream of experience at any scale we desire.

Our forms are programmed to harmony — the other twenty percent of our DNA is not necessarily entangled with consciousness. Seven percent is made up of harmony, frequency, and vibration. The remaining thirteen percent corresponds to how the spiritual codes and contracts unfold in linear and non-linear time, what agencies we work or don't work with, and how no-time beings can consciously entangle with the time-based you to create a brand new contract that is needed for change, auditing of the self.

To use our DNA instrument to the fullest capacity, to tap into our skills, we need to stop giving away our core energy. Instead of preserving and tapping into our source energy connection we keep using the background electromagnetic frequencies to stay motivated — the white noise of our spiritual ghetto. There are so many voices now, echoing through our heads like a hundred tourists visiting an echo chamber in the Grand Canyon — self-help nonsense with no understanding of the deeper strata of consciousness and existence; an endless parade of hawkers projecting their bellowing pitch in the thoroughfare, stocks, bonds, cryptos, minerals, security, prosperity, success, family narratives of fear and doubt inherited by unconscious epigenetic propagation; a million and one voices echoing through the consciousness of the twenty-first century man and woman. How do we ever hear the silence?

There comes a point where the living algorithm of life transcends into the ocean of consciousness. How do we get there anchored down by the consciousness minutia of our time, a time of vast technological advancement that has increased rather than decreased the burden of survival? Only humanity, alone among creatures on this planet, works against its own best interest or can be persuaded to do so quite easily. We're not an equation. We're not just binary numbers. We're so much more than that. The broken man, the man on the cross, has been the template for some time, and it's still working today. It's not who or what we are. The fetish of deconstruction has poisoned the world. We are a holistic creation, the human being, living in a holistic system we voluntarily left under the blindness of trauma. Science, cosmology, economics, and spirituality should have been unified generations ago.

Our environment does not activate us by itself. This is the free will choice of the sentient being. It has to be in our fate, our fetus planning, to even kindle the curiosity to look at the invisible webs of creation. Sooner or later we are taken within to complete the journey to knowledge. External sources can provide the initial catalyst — a book, a retreat, encountering an awakened person, initiation into spiritual practice, or plant propelled journeys into the fourth and fifth dimensions, ayahuasca, peyote, mushrooms, or any other number of chemical to light stimulants in various shamanic cultures throughout the earth — but none may be considered a path unto themselves, and they must be abandoned once they have proved out. Yes, there are other dimensions. Now choose a path, a discipline, a practice, and earn it.

Modern DNA Manipulation

What has happened on this planet is almost unbelievable. In the context of the divine hologram, we need to see the good and the bad. We need to choose. These are standard conceptions of growth and maturity even in psychology. The shocking part is how deep the story of deception goes. When the negative species took over the farm they dumbed humanity down. This happened around seventy-five thousand years ago, long past the time wars, well into the time chaos we live within now.

The cerebellum in the medulla oblongata at the back of the brainstem is now part of the autonomic nervous system. It was not always so. It used to be called the tiny backup brain. There are reptilian species that have two and three brains because of their giant bodies. The cerebellum was implemented into skinsuits to impede evolution — our journey to light and being — and to prevent us from performing rituals and ceremonies which would have shed light on the fake masters and gods years ago.

Medicine was brought into this hologram at the beginning of the Industrial Revolution to stunt our growth and support the global narrative's distortion and distraction. They don't want us to remember our true nature. In ancient times the hologram was very different. The global narrative was based on what the *gods* told us. The cerebellum is the limiting factor for faith itself. The master DNA creators incorporated the cerebellum into the DNA by adding a rung, like creating a new organ, so we would not progress beyond certain experiences and awaken to the fact we're farmed. Our motor cortex used to be actively in alignment with our heart, brain, and gut. Now the cerebellum is completely integrated into our heart-brain-gut complex and interacts as a medium with our reality keeping us in a fight, flight, or freeze state. This is a catatonic state for consciousness expansion. The cerebellum can hinder us from having astral travel experiences. We can overwrite the cerebellum with heart-based meditation. This turns off the medulla oblongata. A superhighway between the brain and heart lights up. This is natural for human beings.

The sphenoid bone is the one with the great wings, just behind the eye sockets, below the frontal bone. It joins many of the other bones in the skull. When working on the sphenoid bone in Cranio Sacral Therapy (CST), we impact the other bones in the skull and the face. The sphenoid bone was radically manipulated so that our residual image would alter during our emotional journeys. When we are depressed our eye sockets are influenced through the sphenoid bones, the ears, the mandibles, the jaw position, how the sinuses are affected, and how much air comes in and out of the nose. The sphenoid bone was manipulated and integrated into the facial structure so we wear our emotions on our sleeves. It allows programs to take over sympathetic and parasympathetic control. Sphenoid alignment is one of the greatest emotional releases we can have. It interlinks with the parietal, temporal, and zygomatic in the cheekbones. In CST when we hold the occiput, and we feel for the movement of the sphenoid bone, people with imbalances there are usually suffering. It is the gyroscope of the face which is linked to a residual image. It's also linked to our capacity to be in the body and recognize our residual image.

Our inner ear bones determine how we hear the tones in our reality. Some people are tone-deaf. Our early infant journey determines how robust these bones grow as we are aligned to the space-time motion and our spiritual center of gravity. The size of these bones has been greatly reduced. They should be four times the size. This hinders our connection to sound and motion. One of the tiniest bones in the ear is the stirrup bone. If bones in the ears were bigger we'd be more spiritually centered. Programs would have less power over us.

The eyelashes keep dirt out and protect the eyes, but they're also antennas just like cat whiskers. We cannot always see them as we blink, but they're very much part of our visionary spiritual journey. Just like cats use their whiskers as a sensing system, we use our eyelashes to assist us psychically. Our tongue and eyelashes have been modified to allow the cerebellum to take control over motion action. If they were not directly hijacked, we'd be able to see all the other layers of reality.

Hair follicles are antennas too. Each different skinsuit has a different quality to hair. Our hair today when cut is dead. In the past, it stayed alive. Alpaca hair under the microscope is alive. The tubes allow light to continuously refract through them. Our hair should be the same way. In the military, they shave off men's hair to be able to control them better. The wind talkers, the native Americans, had thick long hair. It helped decode messages of the wind using light language. Eyelash hair allows us to input data from other realities. The hair as a system has been hijacked by the cerebellum. Hair is linked to our scalp. The scalp is related to the central location system of our file tree. Many people have a round bald patch on top of their heads. That says their DNA is limiting parts of their crown chakra.

The funny bone inside the elbow is a big nerve ganglion that has grown out of proportion to impact how the skeletal system interacts with the vagus nerve. It bypasses the skeletal system, so we feel more through the flesh than the bones. When our bones and hair are in sympathetic alignment, we get the feeling of our hair standing up at the back of our neck. They increased the funny bone size so it was more data-oriented than the other bones. By being more aware of the muscle than the bone, we gain strength faster and can lift heavy loads. This is how the manipulation through the cerebellum sourced and maintained the slave communities.

At one point, the DNA skinsuit could switch from male to female at will. Men's nipples remained because they couldn't remove them when they started modifying our bodies towards procreation, as opposed to recreation. In the past pleasure was another form of control. It's making something of a comeback in the late twentieth and early twenty-first centuries.

We're the technology of the founders. We're supposed to be self-entertaining, self-educating, and self-evolving, but this is in context to our environment, and this includes our inner environment, our thoughts, and beliefs. The global narrative is now, and has been for some time, the context within which our innate abilities grow and adapt. The problem is that the environment is false. True DNA does not know how to express the truth in a false context. The Adam's apple is another control system to limit men's sovereignty. It works through the projection of the voice during the *I am* evolution at puberty. The loss and gain of innocence were controlled in the DNA through the lineages.

We have thirty-three vertebrates in the spine instead of forty. The side wings of the vertebrates should be a more robust expression. Our spinal column has fewer vertebrates and they're bigger. We should have smaller ones and seven more with greater space in between the vertebrates to allow more plasticity of the body itself. With fewer vertebrates, it's easier to become bogged down with depression programs. In some off-world DNA skinsuits, they have seventy-two vertebrates and a greater brain processing power. Each vertebrate is a part of the brain stem connected to the vagus nerve and cerebellum. If you take out the cerebellum, the entire skeletal spinal column is an extension of the brain. More vertebrates allow more interaction with the chakras beyond the crown. Giraffes have the bigger processing power, just like the Brontosaurus that had a ninety-foot long neck.

Our eyes and our third eye have been manipulated, too. The function of the third eye and our pineal gland is hijacked by the cerebellum at birth. Once you cut the umbilical cord, the cerebellum takes over the special awareness instead of having the third eye remain in charge of awareness until puberty. A baby with the third eye engaged at birth without cutting the cord would have a radically different perceptive capacity.

Our eye color is an aspect of the DNA and is directly connected to the residual image. A child can choose its eye color by changing it in the first few months. It's flowing through the Cranio Sacral system, projecting light out the eyes through the lens of their color.

The thymus gland has been manipulated also. It still goes back to the cerebellum implant. If you take the cerebellum out all of those manipulated and corrupted capacities would return to normal. At this stage of our development, the cerebellum cannot be surgically removed without rendering the patient brain dead. Due to the holographic reality we live in, some people have sixty percent of their brains gone because of an accident and they're still alive and aware.

The appendix was originally to help process vegetable matter that was very difficult to break down. The function of the appendix is not greatly understood now and it's often removed. It still helps to balance the gut gnome to dampen candida, amplify other microorganisms, and put nutrients into the gut system to support digestion.

The tonsils were a filtration system for airborne bacteria. They close off the air passageway to the lungs and act as a portal for fluid, like gills, for other atmospheric-type journeys. Depending on the skinsuit, it can change the sound of the voice when removed, where removal might impact on the potency of voice projection.

In certain DNA skinsuits, wisdom teeth have to come out for the jaw to function. Those are modifications to limit the body. They will rot if you don't extract them. Dentistry was typically a death sentence in the past. The name *wisdom* tooth itself is a play and imprint on the belief system. The teeth are intricately linked to the nervous system, a vital part of what goes into our gut. Teeth help us to relate to our residual images. Some people can gain more of their reality through a set of fake teeth. Heavy metal fillings, like mercury, create a bio-electric frequency that distorts all of the nerve endings and the chemical reactions in the dental system. Teeth are often connected to entities. They hijack the gut through the teeth.

The shape of the organs is determined by the size of the vertebrates. More and smaller vertebrates would impact the organs. Everybody's skinsuit has different shapes of organs. This is the medical industry's deep, dark secret. Many people have *upside down organs* – literally. It's not a DNA flaw. It's just like consciousness in the DNA lineage is organized differently to allow a different experience. The organs are shaped differently depending on the skinsuit. The organ positions do not change our consciousness being in the vagus nerve or the sympathetic and parasympathetic nervous system. Many DNA skinsuits off the earth have a second heart in the intestinal tract which creates extended peristalsis. The cerebellum becomes another heart, controlling the micro-pressure of blood flowing through the brain, allowing brain, heart, gut coherence. The heart is the first organ, the tongue is second, the third is our lymph system, the thymus, the fourth, and the fifth are the gut and heart.

Our environment interacts with the DNA instruments through the pineal gland. Fluorides create a crystalline structure in the fluid sac of the pineal gland. The purpose of this crystalline structure is to take scalar wave information from etheric satellites to influence our local dreamtime in sacred geometry cities. Transformers on the light poles along the streets can create an omnidirectional field that interacts with the crystals in our pineal gland to keep us trapped outside global dreamtime. The plugs in our room, our TV sets, computers, routers, and many other deliberately designed devices create an electromagnetic field to suppress the pineal gland. Decalcification of the pineal gland is a good thing.

Fertility and Spirituality

Fertility is another area of gross manipulation, as well. There's an eye in the heart. It's often activated through childbirth. Women can see through this eye in the same manner we see through the third eye in the forehead. The menstrual cycle is a way for the rods and cones to align with the third eye plus the ones in the heart, rectum, or clitoris, all extensions of the third eye. A man's third eye can travel to the tip of the penis and connect into the womb portal from there. Menstrual cramps and pains are often a sign of being out of alignment in those areas. A most beneficial prayer technique for women during their cycle is to call in all their thoughts, ideas, constructs, and energies from previous menstruation cycles and detach from them on a month-to-month basis. These powerful times for women are being hijacked and bastardized by the global narrative. The menstrual blood is very powerful as the energy of being a negotiator, an arbitrator, or peacemaker.

Menstruation continues after menopause. Women still go through the cycle without blood. The fertility spirits attached to menopause move on to a higher density. The DNA is no longer producing the unique experience of bleeding, but the spiritual mechanics remain the same, even more intensified through menopause. In most cases, when women experience heavy menopausal symptoms, they're giving birth in other simultaneous realities which need the births. Their remaining fertile life alters versions of themselves who did not get pregnant. Using their biological clock, they find a signature frequency match to complete interdimensional birthing as part of their karmic resolution.

Hot flashes can happen when an alternate version of the woman is breaking water and is more than likely going to die from birth. They transfer chemical life force based on their experience to avoid this. A hot flash can also be another version of us in another place and time, and in an alien form, in which the birth got difficult. Birthing is part of the karmic resolution. This is important to remember. Through strands of awareness in the DNA, the connective tissues transfer life force to assist in that birth by another simultaneous version of ourselves who lacks fertility power or lives in an environment with no fertility at all. This allows the mystical births to happen, the babies who should never have survived or lived. Evening primrose oil is one of the natural remedies for hot flashes. This plant oil is harvested as an essence to lessen the effect in this reality and, at the same time, it amplifies the experience on the unseen side.

Some strands in the DNA need a special chemical soup in the body to activate fertility. It used to be manipulated in the overall chemistry of the body. Other strands had more opportunities to awaken. When a woman who never gave birth is going through a very difficult time during menopause, another version of her simultaneous existence is going through a birthing experience. They are both intrinsically linked to reducing the negative effect. There are times when co-living souls go through menopause together. This generates new life in celestial nurseries. It gives birth to a new soul frequency in the ocean of awareness. The new soul frequency begins the journey into the sea of consciousness and manifests in time and space.

The fatty deposit around the midline during menopause serves as a protective membrane, but it can block good experiences with regards to working with a woman's residual image. Once the biological fertility clock stops ticking, the *awareness clock* takes over. We can gain a greater awareness and perspective of the awakening. We can experience mood swings when the body is trying to find the right chemistry. It's a balance between overproducing and underproducing hormones and chemicals.

Men go through menopause too, and they also have their process through cycles of creation. As they actualize their physical manifestations, a house, artwork, business, what have you, they leave their legacy for their clan, tribe, nation, or zeitgeist. Men build an archive of experience that stays manifested in time and space. Lineages in the unseen can plan lives through the infrastructure created by the urge of manifestation.

Men reach their sexual peak around the age of eighteen, women in their thirties. This is why the infrastructure in the unseen needs to be planned. The cycles have been manipulated by DNA farming. If the human reproductive cycle was not manipulated, most pregnancies would be eighteen to twenty-four months. In some instances, it can be up to five years. In the past, the umbilical cord wouldn't be cut for months. This allowed more bonding between the partners. There was more opportunity for the father to have a ritual connection to the child through the mother as the medium of the connection.

Testosterone drives creativity in men. There are other things similar to testosterone that drive construction. A male scientist does not use testosterone, but he uses another version of it, a mental aspect of testosterone. There's no scientific name for it yet in this reality. There are several hundred forms of testosterone, each with a different chemical chain that allows a different aspect of creation. Through manipulation of our bodies, we are not producing the all-encompassing testosterone which keeps us in fight, flight, or freeze. Our glands have been manipulated to produce one strand of testosterone over the other which leads us back to the cerebellum in the motor cortex.

The birth control pill is manufactured from giant farms of female horses. The urine of a pregnant horse is the chemical basis of the birth control pill. The horses are pregnant their entire life. Their colts are taken and chopped up into horse meat and sold to pet food manufacturers and fast-food restaurants. The entire industry revolves around the urine of pregnant horses for human birth control pills.

Many women reject the different types of pills. There's a malaise associated with the pill they can feel. They become worse and worse until they get the birth control pill out of their lives. Before the horse urine birth control pill, there were plenty of natural herbal remedies to stop pregnancy. Like most lineage medicine — Ayurveda, traditional Chinese medicine, homeopathy, naturopathy — it was delegitimized and marginalized by the big allopathic medical footprint that coincided with the big push into the twentieth-century economy, in which everything was patented, synthetically replicated, restricted to *licensed* practitioners, taxed and brought into the mercantile system. This was an ancillary component of the imprinted global narrative at the beginning of the Industrial Revolution.

The I Am Individuation Process

Every moment within a time-space equation creates an energetic imprint that cannot be erased. We're always painting on the canvas with the sound and light in our heads. Even thoughts are recorded, states of mind, emotions, not just actions. We're always creating. Self-mastery is creating in full consciousness. Sovereignty is full responsibility for every thought, word, and deed. There are no splitting hairs on this point. The new age movement proselytizes intentional co-creation in faux ritual, basically wish-fulfillment. Everybody buys into it, this dumbed-down version of the co-creation absent self-mastery. It's a recipe for disaster, a moron's guide to magical malpractice beginning with the state of mind.

No two physical objects occupy space simultaneously. There is no simultaneous or identical history as they follow a unique light path. We are a standing sine wave of existence as the *I am* apex in the incarnated now, in resonance or dissonance with our previous and future source streams. The quantum hologram carries the complete history of each energetic imprint of all source streams within this timeline paradox.

We have mighty *I am* selves in the past where we were extremely powerful energy being compared to what we are now. As part of the karmic resolution, we gave away our *I am* self-sovereignty to conduct timeline recovery operations. Those ancient *I ams*, plus another forty to fifty *I am* selves spread all over timelines and dimensions, are still making decisions that can alter our present choices. This is one reason why so many people are unsuccessful in this present world. When we have two or more present selves making choices in a free-will universe, one choice contradicts the other. We cancel ourselves out at the co-creator level.

There is another level of paradox in which we have one present self on high energy earth and another present self on very low energy earth. One can easily dominate from high or low energy. Reclaiming our sovereignty reclaims our authority from all high-energy versions of ourselves in competition and hierarchy. It removes our citizenship from all involved organizations. All our shards, parts, and avatars can leapfrog forward in time and claim unity consciousness to remedy all paradoxes.

When we transit timelines, we must figure out which is optimal for us. It can also be involuntary. We could call this a form of harvesting. We can get deliberately thrown off our timeline, or we can have chunks taken out of us and put into different timelines. This sounds fanciful, but remember, our DNA is technology. Entire ancestral lineages have been harvested like this for eons of time.

A point comes when the harvesting ends. We must make a final choice to be here and now with our friends and family. A scenario like this would be planned before birth. It is often facilitated through a traumatic experience in this lifetime. It gets us to the timeline we need to be on. A good way of working through such traumas and dramas is to look at a photo album. Get in touch with us at the various stages of our lives. Bring memories to the surface and look for pattern recognition. People are often born onto the wrong timeline. The soul knows it. It has to go through trials and tribulations to get back to where it needs to be. The dreaming body — the main time-traveling technology for us – facilitates those changes.

The mighty *I am* apex presence co-creating self has come into this world now as a representation of all our sentient selves which incarnated into this world before with decision making power for all the celestial minds of our past, present, and future lives. Only the ever-present mighty *I am* self in the now can make choices in co-creation with the unity consciousness world. In other words, the *I am* apex presence of the now is the ultimate choice mechanism of this lifetime. Other aspects of our self can provide the information upon which we make choices. The ever-presence is all of our other selves in dominion with the *I am* presence now resolving contracts with soul family, soul planets, or whatever else we are experiencing in this reality. We, as the *I am* apex presence, are deeply honored by all the ancestors because we are in an ongoing co-creation with the world to expand consciousness as a global community of transformers and consciousness explorers.

The essence of this universe is free will of the *I am* presence now. The soul and higher self are included, but the higher self does not get to make choices, only the *I am* presence does here and now. The higher self can counsel but it can't give us the questions, only the answers. When our history is eliminated, it puts us in the paradox of paradoxes. We don't understand who we truly are. We may not even have any questions to ask. This is often an indication that there are parts of ourselves making decisions for us without us involved. Those paradoxes can be forty or fifty *I ams* at the time working on destruction rather than evolution. We can't destroy other *I ams*, but we can work with them. We can heal them, or we can ban them through our free will choices and actions within the authority as this *I am* apex presence of the now.

We are already the higher self. The *I am* is here in time, as constructed by the higher self during womb planning, and the higher self is holographically interacting with you at all times. The *I am* here and now is based on several previous *I am* selves who have gone through life reviews and set up a theme of karma or dharma for this lifetime. In the first five years or so we fully activate our *I am* technology. The rest of the *I am* comes in during puberty. Our higher self remains the sacred neutral observer throughout all our incarnations. When we die, we meet our higher self again as ten thousand past and future generations of other selves. The *I am* is the technology of interface with the God source already in us. We have to learn to get to know ourselves as the embodied spiritual human to understand our soul's purpose and missions.

Precognitive Workforce

The *I am* precognitive workforce is all versions of ourselves at the same time. Nobody ever speaks about future lives. Why not? Why are all the religions end-of-the-line trains? Why do none of them discuss the continuity of life? Why is every path on this planet a thinly veiled prison break? Why are they all so contemptuous of the earth? Do we even realize how long we have been breeding contempt for life? What a happy place to begin a lifetime — this place sucks, but the next place will be better. There is no next place not born out of the trials of this place. They are two versions of the same thing at different frequencies, one so dense and domineering it blunts the other. Mythology is the bridge between here and there. It was always literal. That's why this new mythology of the galactic historian is as literal as possible. The age of metaphor and allegory is over. All the ciphers are deciphered already. That's another part of what the event did. We're so used to not knocking on the doors of the next world we don't even remember if anything might open the door. Now is the time to knock again.

When the global narrative ramped up with the Industrial Revolution, the separation between the subject and the object increased. Mythology fused it all like a poetic container, but mythology was rendered impotent by the Industrial Revolution. It just happened so fast, from the outhouse to nuclear power in the blink of an eye, with only two world wars to clear the path. That's quite amazing. Change and violence are symbionts in time. They coexist in the same times, places, and circumstances – always. The faster the change, the greater the violence. The global narrative has been written in blood. They never needed ink, but they sure like it.

The global narrative made us forget about the other side, our doors to it, and our birthright to at least know it, if for no other reason than to transcend the fear of death, and that's what the old mythologies did – they conquered death. Nobody is saying that's the end of it. It goes on almost infinitely, but overcoming death is the first step toward a new construct with new riddles. Death is the main riddle of this third dimension. In some eras of humanity, we lived in full knowledge of the life and death process, the golden age and the silver age had no death. The body ended but they knew it was not the end of them — knew, not believed — and that was the difference. The dark ages of man, and we are coming out of a very dark age now, some of us will anyway, not everyone — very important to remember that — are periods of low consciousness for man. That's what all the violence has been about. It stuns consciousness and puts it under a blanket of trauma. Trauma is undigested consciousness. We can not see clearly until we have digested it. The underlying truth of religion has been — *get out of here.* It's fundamentally right, but we're not going anywhere. We have to get out of the false world we were conscripted into co-creating, the beliefs, lies, and superstitions that have proliferated under the global narrative, the rank filth of these programmed limitations. We were created to know things, not believe them.

The final solution for consciousness as written by the global narrative is depression, self-loathing, and self-immolation. Bad human. Into your crate. Your behavior has destroyed the earth. Rampant use of fossil fuels, which you had no choice but to use because it was the underpinning of the global narrative's economy, has brought us to the brink of extinction, which just happens to coincide with end times in all major religions in one half of the world, a kind of secular apocalypse if you will, but potent in striking fear into the heart. That's the whole point, to throw off the compass of the heart because the heart is the only instrument that can navigate us out of the global narrative and back to celestial mediumship. That's why there's been so much violence, so much change, and so much fear in the heart. When the collective heart is full of fear the world inverts. Rather than create the universal template of beauty, we create ugliness. We murder more babies than we birth. We become denser by our systems of education rather than lighter. Everything inverts. It's part of the binary system in which we live. They know it. They can flip it like a fuse box.

Our precognitive workforce has been limited by a global narrative that corrodes our ability to believe in ourselves. It's such a ridiculous thing on its face — belief in yourself — but it's true. We are so far removed from any semblance of being human we have been reduced to *believing in ourselves*, you know, like a salmon needs to believe in itself to swim back to its spawning ground, or a hawk needs to believe it can nosedive to a kill from a thousand meters. It's humiliating to have to believe in ourselves, but here we are, reduced and depleted by DNA manipulation — slave engineering — untold generations of dreamtime blockade, witch burnings, violence, torture, warfare, and trauma. It's no wonder it might be difficult to believe in a precognitive workforce. We stopped believing in ourselves, looking in ourselves, which was the desired effect of the global narrative. There's nothing to believe in. We are far more than we've been taught.

The spiritual is at the far end of the acknowledgment spectrum. Evidence is a compelling case, but, like everything else, it falls prey to the context and details alignment. Yes, gravity is real, but only because it's the consensus. There's never been a generation of human beings that did not produce human beings who could levitate, so yes gravity is real, but only in context to the natural human experience. In the context of the supernatural, gravity is not real. It's just a low law of nature that can be opted out of when we develop. This is not to say that people should drop what they're doing and pursue a life dedicated to the nearly meaningless accomplishment of levitating but do be honest when assessing the law. Gravity is a jurisdictional law. We can go places it has no jurisdiction.

We're more likely to accept a chemical definition, because chemistry is scientific, and science is the soil in which they want to culture scientism, a new religion in which object truth will be the only accepted norm. In the case of dementia, old age for example, where the earliest memories become the most lucid and immediate, and short-term memory becomes more difficult, there's a breakdown of chemical memory association in the file tree. This is where the skull cap — the top of the crown — tells the spirit where all the files are stored inside the body. The chemical memories are corrupting the file tree because the brain itself has broken down through lesions. Cellular pathways don't have the energy to support the brain. There is a breakdown in the genetic journey and part of the life and death contract. In a limited context, chemistry explains dementia, but it doesn't give a full definition, nor does it pretend to know anything about death. There is no science of light. Electromagnetism has shut down for public consumption a long time ago. It would have unified science and spirituality, and it would have proved gravity was a jurisdictional law. That could not be allowed to happen.

Significant distorted memory just before death triggers a markedly different form of life review. Reverting to younger versions of the self is a co-existence in time through bilocation. It skews the light memories. The light body does not identify to a single point of time anymore. This is the corruption of the chemical memory, the time stamping. This disease can be contracted by the fetus in the womb or by DNA design and plan.

There are certain DNA skinsuits with a prevalent experience in them. The fetus knows that before it goes into the DNA form for the experience. There is much we can do to prevent this, but we don't have the proper gut gnome from a very young age to support brain health. The life journey was cut radically short by the manipulation that was done to the DNA about 35,000 years ago when the brain stem was augmented. The motor cortex functions were assigned an earlier ending date than the actual extended life process. This is what has been done to us, difficult to hear but necessary. Many of us could live two to three hundred years if we had proper trauma resolution so as not to burn out the neurological pathways. Optimal gut health is a remedy to avoid plaque build-up which causes dementia. It is all about the volume of individuals who are part of the ocean of awareness choosing to experience law as a fundamental value of experience from one era of light to the next.

Universal laws come down to egg and sperm technology, or other birthing processes that generate lineages differently. The birthing technologies determine how the universal laws are used, and every birthing technology has different quantum laws. The sperm, seed, and egg technology allow access to the infinite blueprint at the planning stage. Sexuality and prayer are built into our DNA. Our DNA is in sympathetic creation with the natural order here. This reality gives us coherent resonance with geometric holograms of information to decode, process, and use to our advantage.

The journey into greater awareness is understanding how to use our energy as a conscious being of choice. We start in this bliss state where the infinite code is in the celestial mediumship. The celestial medium steps down into the fetus and goes through the laws of forgetting so it does not have access to its infinite sight. It then is a part of this hologram as a non-infinite being who is on the journey to celestial mediumship again. We are forever trying to get back to that place of bliss and joy. All the teachings since the dawn of spirituality have blissful teaching. It is our birthright. Inside the fetus in the womb state is the non-locality teaching. We are both locality and non-locality. What makes us different from the fetus are the memories we have stored in light. Our blueprint as a fetus has the infinite set of memories and potentials we've created. The incarnation process allows us to experience all forms of life on the planet. We go through all the forms of life. This is the mastery path in its purest form. The *I am* data unpacks and decodes itself through its eras of incarnation. We add the chemical memories to enforce linear time so spiritual contracts can come to fruition.

Our precognitive workforce is the light world to chemical world bridge. It's another opportunity for science to study spirit, but it's difficult to get a community committed to objective truth to even accept spirit as a noun, after all, it's not a person, place, or thing, but none of them would exist without it. Science is trying to mimic what our mythologies did for us, conquer death, and certainly, the *black* sciences practiced in America and elsewhere, the *Paperclip* science, has traded off-world for anti-aging and regression technology, but without the proper the spiritual context for a longer life, which would be greater surrender and service to the larger purpose of earth, humanity, and our multidimensional reality, new forms of monstrosity can only come about. Use your precognitive workforce. It's there for you.

Precognitive Sharing

Our precognitive workforce is us. It is the understanding we can create infinite conscious versions of ourselves and travel time, future and past, and prepare a resource of knowledge and information we can instantly call upon as manifestations of inspiration to beat anything negative. Our *I am* precognitive workforce has earned the right for cross-time collaboration. There are negative frequencies in this journey. We need to empower ourselves. The *I am* in the here and now declares itself a being of co-creation, absent competition and hierarchy, a dreaming *I am* breakaway DNA light body civilization of one in this life form, the human being. We can use the genuine work to make a great impact on loved ones, family, clan, nation, tribe, and earth mother. If we choose to do this on all scales, we need a masterful precognitive workforce, our birthright, and legacy, to create as a natural co-creative evolutionary being who is part of the great dreamtime awakening. We use our responsibility to impact the loves of our lives, the themes and ideologies we promote to others, a little dreamtime capital so they can find their illumination, free from gurus, without sending them down paths to false illumination. Our precognitive workforce is there waiting to work with us, to think with us, to love with us, to be part of our greater expression. We must put the time, effort, and energy into understanding we can call upon our inner geniuses from many dimensions, time streams, galaxies, and universes to form a forceful collective, all of us, all part of this dreamtime awakening, freeing ourselves from the limitation of the global narrative.

Shamans have always used their precognitive workforce. Every generation learns from the previous. We are a signature frequency match to our precognitive workforce, and to the collective workforce of the highest forms of our light soul teachers, all of the *I am* instances as part of our great hall of Akashic Records.

We tread on someone else's journey if we send out our precognitive workforce to help them in a co-creational way. There's a fine line where too much is too much. If the other being has no precognition, or any form of understanding of what a precognitive workforce is, we are stepping on their journey. Infants or young children who haven't formed an *I am* yet are okay. Most children don't fully form the *I am* until puberty when the thymus gland creates three hundred new chemicals that suddenly flood the body. This is puberty itself. It solidifies the *I am* technology as a time-space equation. When we assist others with our precognitive workforce, we have an interdimensional conversation with them whereby we join our precognitive workforces to create a manifestation of synchronicities. It helps each of the parties co-create an event that brings inspiration and healing. Healers become facilitators. They amalgamate their precognitive workforce with the precognitive workforce of the ill person. The ill person may not have any consciousness skills. If those *I am* beings want to become true consciousness beings of choice they must learn the process of self-illumination. There's an infinite amount of teachers out there in the great dreamtime awakening. Discover what's the signature frequency match for you then go out, evolve, and create.

Our temporal awareness has been manipulated. A lot of weaponized time travel technology interferes with humanity's capacity to perceive time. We can be heavily confused with our temporal awareness. Confusion is an aspect of temporal distortion. It can be sped up or slowed down. Our temporal awareness is unconscious to time speeding up or slowing down. Our temporal awareness determines our perception and perspective on how fast the algorithm can move. Separate from the vagus nerve, the thymus generates temporal awareness between the brain, heart, and gut, then all three separate from unity, making it easier to split consciousness. The connective systems between the thymus, brain, heart, and gut are where we can hijack temporal awareness. That is another limiting system that was put inside us, however, it has backfired on the temporal manipulators. It gives us other *backdoor frequencies* of awareness through the temporal body.

Temporal hijacking has been around since the dawn of time. The whole point of it is to manipulate our capacity to the time stamp. Interlopers discovered the infinite journey of the soul then tried to figure out where, when, and how they might create an incoherent pattern and get a soul trapped in an era of history. They could then generate a global narrative of mass distraction for DNA farming and hinder the *I am* consciousness from again entering the sea of consciousness.

Temporal manipulation started forty-eight to fifty-five thousand years ago. Not all life forms practiced temporal manipulation. It was about limiting the number of life forms on the surface of the earth. Particular DNA lineages were not receptive to this temporal manipulation. We went from nine-hundred thousand different forms to one-hundred and thirty-five thousand. This is the basis of DNA farming. This is how they manipulate and limit who is going to be on the farm.

The apparatus of infinite interconnectivity is the simultaneous existing network of selves. This forms the hub of interconnectivity, part of our precognitive and post cognitive workforce. The unvanquished dream is an aspect of the infinite interconnectivity, giving us an even greater connection to all the versions of ourselves sharing that perspective. The unvanquished dreamer of peace comes in here too. It connects to all the forgotten and remembered oceans of awareness, the many seas of consciousness, layered atop all forms of thought and awareness, to connect them in a single time-space location. It's a state of being that can walk on time.

Mind Heart Gut

It's important to create distinctions, to set things apart, to be specific about things. We've discussed a lot so far. It's all a bit detailed. A little context is required. Our precognitive workforce is in the ocean of awareness, but we have a lot more equipment. A lot of our hardware, our skinsuit, is unknown to us. It's kind of remarkable when you think about it. Deconstruction is our main pastime in the *the enlightenment*. We have modern anatomy because da Vinci dug up bodies and dissected them. Philosophy may not have murdered the wholeness of God, but it certainly helped bury the body, not that it matters; it was a false god anyway. It only marks the last time we lived within mythology, contrived and spiritually dead mythology, but it nailed heaven and earth together well enough for peasants. We're on to nanotechnology, RNA vaccines, CERN cracking into other dimensions with the Large Hadron Collider, but we know the barest of details about ourselves. When we remember the global narrative it all makes sense. When we remember the relentless and brutal suppression of human consciousness, it all makes sense. You can not control an autonomous thing. You can not persuade a spiritually aware being to volunteer for codependency. You can not manufacture consent.

Three parts of a human being pass information — the mind, the heart, and the gut. We say when asked how we know something, *gut*. Everybody knows what we mean — not empirical — a kind of instinct and intuition. The heart is much more verbose in the human record. We attribute the heart to conscience, moral direction, love of the creation and the creator. The heart is a powerful receiver in the human system, and its proper functioning opens up higher communication from the light worlds. It is in many ways a passage between the chemical and light experiences. Many forms of addiction are the result of not wanting to deal with the heart, distilling some feeling of betrayal, or allowing the trauma to dominate the heart.

The mind is information processing and a very powerful receiver itself. It is the easiest part of a human being to trick, control, program, or destroy. The human mind is a fractal of the universal mind, which is all knowledge, as the heart is a fractal of the universal heart, which is unconditional love, and the gut is individual to us except for a network of conscious beings. When the three parts work together, a nearly perfect human information system is operating. Why don't we know that? Why don't we incorporate it into our basic education systems? Well, who would profit from that enterprise? It's amazing how many questions you can answer with that one filter that defines the system logic we live within — who would profit from the enterprise?

Sometimes the mind processes better than the heart, or the gut, or the other way round. Then there are certain pieces of information where the mind, the heart, and the gut have to work together. Once the mind-heart-gut starts working together, the analogical side of the mind – which compares two things — gets stronger, along with the empowered programs that are with it. This is why daily practice is so important. We use the brain to interpret inter-dimensional frequencies of the multiple versions of self. The brain is the instrument of experience. It has a gut-brain and a heart-brain, each with its sense of time.

DNA communicates within the skinsuit. It communicates from form to form through incarnations. It communicates between incarnations. It communicates to our light bodies. It goes from chemical to light. This understanding allows reasoned contemplation on many consequence theologies, the wages of sin, the sins of the father, and karma itself, whether applied to an individual, a family, a community, geography, or any other distribution point; it's all one DNA communication network, the prime creator's backbone for several layers of experience, straddling light and chemical, which correlates to the physical body and the light body. We are simultaneously living *I am* versions of ourselves, scattered through time. In low consciousness these other selves are unrecognized. In higher consciousness, our awareness permits communication to multiple selves through precognitive sharing, the consciousness of the earth itself, and multiple races of beings from other worlds in other parts of the galaxy and universe.

The *I am*, as the incarnate life form, occupies and entangles consciousness within the body through three stages. One, the consciousness is in the brain-heart-gut. The brain-heart-gut complex links to the central nervous system. The central nervous system connects the entire fascia system through the vagus nerve — the central nervous system connector — as part of the DNA communication system. Two, consciousness is in the sympathetic nervous system (SN) and the parasympathetic nervous system (PSN). Three, consciousness is in the entire neural pathway network, fascia, dermis, hairs, the entire system. It connects to the gallbladder which is intraconnected to the vagus nerve. Every organ is intraconnected and interconnected to the vagus nerve.

The skinsuit is part of the individual and collective experience. Our life forms are on all different levels of awareness — planetary, solar, galactic, and universal. Contemplate the vagus nerve aligned to our magnetic North and South Pole. The sympathetic and parasympathetic are our local space-time. The sympathetic drives our daily actions when the soul is in the body. The parasympathetic drives the body in lucid dreaming and other spiritual states, or when it is fully in self-defeating programs. The sympathetic can also be self-defeating and kick the spirit out of the body. It's driven to resolve karma. It guides us like a compass to choose a variety of karma out of the free will. The vagus nerve is connecting to the North Pole, our ancestors, and to the South Pole, our future generations. We need to reclaim the vagus nerve as the truest spiritual sovereign authority we have. Parasympathetic and sympathetic programs can kick us out of the body. A sympathetic example would be road rage, rebellious energy for the most part. When the parasympathetic takes over and thinks it is the soul, the ego and the shadow have allied with each other to manifest an internal villain, a bully, so the soul can't be in the body. In Jung's psychology the subconscious looks upon the sympathetic as fight, flight, or freeze, and it looks upon the parasympathetic as rest, digest, and relax.

Entanglement is the measure of how much consciousness is in control of the body. It is measured through the vagus nerve, the sympathetic nervous system, and the parasympathetic nervous system. The subconscious rest, digest, and relax vagus nerve connection is when we are in those spiritual moments where we are reclaiming our authority, taking back our power, and purging the vagus nerve. Once we fully occupy the central vagus nerve with our consciousness, we can flow it directly into the sympathetic and parasympathetic nervous system. This is how the incarnate life form can retain lucid dream creations. This explains why people run by programs have difficulty lucid dreaming. It's difficult to make rich, high-quality memories. The vagus nerve and the parasympathetic are connected to mystical experiences. The sympathetic has neural pathways designed to use the five senses. The five senses sum to the sixth sense, the totality of the experience.

Think of a violin. The parasympathetic system is the body of the violin. The sympathetic system is analogous to the strings on the violin. The vagus nerve is the bow. Consciousness plays the violin. The consciousness of the earth itself is the conductor. The parasympathetic system is the resonance chamber. These things are useless alone. The string is nothing without the bow. The vibration is nothing without the hollow chamber resonating with the body of the violin. The fine-tuning relates to how much the soul is in the body.

The consciousness of the planet hands out the sheet music, the larger composition to which the individual instruments contribute — the blueprint of synchronicities. The planet is the interconnection so the skinsuit can have an experience with the planet. This may be alone, with individual family members, cultures, religions, anything in the sheet music provided by the consciousness of the planet. In this orchestration, we seek harmony to make direct signature frequency matches. The planet simultaneously exists in the ocean of awareness and the sea of consciousness. The planet's celestial mind is the medium between these two levels of awareness, as well as the planet itself, manifested in time and space so that beings living inside it can have a set of unique experiences. This applies to every planet in the universe, with only a few exceptions. The celestial mind of the planet is intraconnected with the celestial mind of us, the life forms, as well as intraconnected with the ocean of awareness and the sea of consciousness manifesting in physical and non-physical space.

We want vagus nerve, sympathetic, and parasympathetic sovereignty. This permits intraconnection and interconnection to our celestial minds. The journey is in maintaining sovereign connection as an ongoing experience until the experience is second nature. At this unfoldment, we can achieve other forms of embodiment. We can leave the body and not lose control of the three aspects of consciousness entanglement. We can create versions of ourselves in other places, spaces, and times. This is our legacy as multidimensional and multi-functional beings. We can adapt the form to communicate with other places, spaces, and species. Sovereignty is earned when the soul can leave at will.

DNA was designed so when we reach a certain frequency we are no longer solely within the chemical experience. Chemical exchanges are fundamental to the life forms living in this third density. Our journey is from chemical to light. The water — the fluids — that comprise the atoms of our bodies becomes a resonant amplifier. Light-based experiences happen through the refraction of water. The soul is the light inside the body. The water and fluid are refracting it by chemical reaction. When we shine light through water or a prism, there is no chemical separation of the prism of light. Thoughts can be implicate and explicate at the same time — orgasmic experiences, love, and fundamental experience without thought.

The entire experience of death is set to change. Our lives will go to three hundred years, five hundred, seven hundred years in one go. The passing over experience will persist to finish this era of light's karmic accounts. Our capacity to plan future lives with twenty to thirty percent of our life memories, hundreds of millions of years as our database for mapping future lives.

We're not put on our mother's heart for days after birth with the umbilical cord connected. This is the natural law of harmony. Birthing in hospitals with *licensed* medical personnel and limited bedtime due to economies of utility does not complete the first synchronizing of the child. Our *I am* technology has to come out quickly in our body in the present system. Everything is set to slow down. The future will see more natural birthing. Pregnancy will be between nine and twenty-five months.

There are children here now with a good part of their memory available to them. They might be ahead of time and lack parental guidance. The fetus in the womb planning is set to change as well. The mother and father will co-plan the spiritual journey before the fetus even enters the womb. It will be light-based planning from the outset while fully incarnate in this third density. This is multidimensional living. This is the great leap forward, no offense to Mao Zedong. He had the concept right. It was the context he lacked. A whole new human race is ready to step out of the chrysalis of time and spread its magnificent and colorful wings. This is the promise.

Part II

Humanity and the Milky Way

T
E
E

Chapter 3

Self Mastery

Awakening Journey

We live on a seventh-dimensional seed planet. Earth can teleport itself through time and space and seed worlds. These seeded worlds created by our planet, earth, are blank sheets. They have no Akashic Record. The life force seeded by earth allows the new world to start growing with its Akashic Record.

When we reconnect with the source, we become celestial mediums of peace. We start using the womb chakras to create. This was earth's original plan. This planet seeds life and brings the celestial minds into the planet to bond within the solar system. The celestial mind extends spiritual contracts to a sun. The sun extends its contracts to the life force. This connects it to the galactic celestial commerce market.

Awakening is kindling of the awareness strand of galactic commerce through celestial minds, using celestial mediums as the guides and guideposts of the many frequencies of time. This allows the ocean of awareness to go into the sea of consciousness and generate incarnations and reincarnations within a solar system. A solar system is an energetic or a physical being within a world, there to experience the strands of connectivity.

The earth was created for the unique experience of spawning new galaxies. That was the design and intent. The opposite has occurred.

The earth was heavily manipulated into becoming a DNA farm through the time travel wars. Source connection became the greater mission. Our sound and light fractal, our dimension, was hacked. We were set upon the worship of false gods. They have been numerous and continue to this day. It's no coincidence that a spiritual leap forward has begun in the age of technology, even though science itself is godless and the global narrative is anti-god right now. It's the change itself, the gap between the two programs, that allows the window to open a little on our reality. The misdirection or harvesting of human intentional energy is the basis of false fractals of the divine hologram. It's a multidimensional expression of building our prison. We are co-creators. Even if we've forgotten that they haven't. Our intentional energy is a harvested resource, psychic equity in dimensions we pretend don't exist.

Our mission is to experience the infinite ways the soul connects and disconnects from the source. Earth offers a vast variety of messages and concepts to learn soul disconnection. As we disentangle from the system of domination and control, from past lives gone awry, the more we can step into the understanding of true soul connection. There are people on earth who planned hundreds of lives to be here now to assist with this process. We can call this the resistance of free earth. They're here to find the soul codes among all of our species and complete them. Domination and control could no longer keep us separate as soul families with a complete soul code.

The consciousness outside of time we can call the ocean of awareness – the universal hologram — and it has the individual universal experience within. The universal experience becomes a being on a planet who slips into forgetfulness to experience finitude within a larger evolution. The consciousness flow in the ocean of awareness allows the data to go from wave to particle, the celestial medium to the DNA experience. The ocean of awareness is the implicate order. There are different oceans of awareness in other universes, many implicate orders, as every universe creates different agendas, experiences, incarnations, and reincarnations. Not every universe uses incarnation. Many don't use *I am* technology like ours with seed and egg technology.

The ocean of awareness is part of the intricate waveform to which quantum physics refers. It can be collapsed into particles. Every particle can again be broken down into sub-points of observation. The particle can be one DNA lineage and all DNA lineages simultaneously based on what we choose to observe through it. The ocean of awareness generates one particle which is technically the whole hologram, but we perceive the hologram at different levels of awareness. The particle can be tens of millions of lineages and tens of billions of worlds. An individual observer works up the scale of observation that says: I am in this lineage that is this particle on this planet, but it is also part of a solar system, and this makes it a bigger particle, and this fractal expands. Our local hologram is one particle. We are particles inside one particle. As individual particles, we can perceive the next particle – the solar system particle.

There's a specific fetus agenda from lifetime to lifetime. The *avatar* agenda evolves the greater soul's ability to generate light and have experiences over thousands and thousands of *I am* expressions who have been fetuses. There are times where the over-soul – the avatar — gets looped in servitude to a system that lowers its capacity to use light, and, as a result, it cannot expand.

A non-agenda being occurs when time is irrelevant to the great experience. Linear time is not the focus of the agenda. It may do one thing twenty-eight thousand years ago, seventeen things two years ago, two million things forty-eight million years ago, and that, technically speaking, is a non-agenda. The things done in the non-agenda create a resolution for some agendas or apply potential solutions for agendas stuck and unable to move forward. Non-agenda allows us to cut and paste time-based experiences out of certain *I am* experiences and use them temporarily in a new *I am* expression to manifest past or future non-agenda aspects into a present agenda.

Agencies

Agency is a fascinating word. It's a third party that facilitates exchanges between other parties. In the early twentieth century, agencies normalized. They had always been around, but the province of kings and emperors only. An ambassador is a form of the agent, brokering for the centralized power it represents, nation, empire, region, or province. Most of us didn't engage with agencies before the great leap forward in the global narrative — the Gutenberg press plate from the fourth dimension — the Industrial Revolution. Now they affect our lives profoundly. Agency was taken up by the global narrative in full vigor. We have advertising agencies, public relations agencies, the agency around a leader, mitigating decisions and influencing outcomes with counsel and diplomacy. Agency is everywhere now. Most people might think agencies are human inventions. They are not. Like all things we bring into manifestation, they are existing aspects of the multidimensional reality we exist within. The utility and function of causal agencies are the same as terrestrial agencies — a third party that facilitates exchanges between other parties.

Cosmic agencies are made from energies of existences outside of time and the *I am*, which is finite in time, as each instance of an *I am* is finite. It's part of the incarnation package. Our past lives are *I am* instances. Agencies work with the *I am*. They're kind of like non-physical bureaucracies. It's quite astounding the bureaucracy on the other side. The dimensions can be a regulatory nightmare. The bureaucracies we have on earth — large corporations, departments and ministries, police and military, almost everything in the modern world — is a reflection of an internal multidimensional bureaucracy. As above so below. The cosmic agencies facilitate karma resolution. They close contracts.

Remember what we have discussed already in this book. Karma is any utility of energy to manifest, prepare to manifest — as in thought – feelings which demand manifestation, and, of course, actions, which, in a conscious person at least, are the product of thought and feeling. Incarnation is all about contracts and karma. It's planned out in the fetus in the womb. Agencies facilitate the contracts. If you come from another spiritual tradition, perhaps it's best to regard them as agents of the lords of karma, or, in a Western model, the agents of fate and destiny. It's important to understand our full self-responsibility as sovereign beings. We are responsible for everything we think, feel, and manifest, where manifestation is the fulfillment of creation, tying off the inner and outer worlds, the imagination and reality.

Agencies are not always operating at the highest standards and practices when compared to something like the precognitive workforce. Let's say we have a chunk of karma that has to be resolved at a high frequency. We have to work with low-quality agencies to resolve karma. We can terminate cooperation with an agency and agents outside agencies. Culture is an external factor that influences the themes of agencies and agents. The agency is our first point of contact when we are a fetus in the womb. Together with our higher self, it is responsible for creating all spiritual contracts for this lifetime. The employer of the agency is the human, the *I am* of this lifetime. The employees — agents of the agency — are the various *I ams* who represent the many expressions of us in the unseen, so we are our agency, a compendium of past and future *I am* expressions, just another testament to the power and creativity of this creation, and how we are very much a part of it at all stages and expression, the only variable being our awareness of it.

Agencies don't always work in unison. They're subject to the same power plays we see on the earth. They sometimes try to take over the agency. Us of today was once a fetus in our mother's womb. The fetus knows it needs a variety of experiences to plan infinite potentials. It works hand in hand with the agency to make a series of contracts that fit our karmic resolution. The more efficient the agency works, the more often we reuse it through our many fetus plans. Some of them are low-quality agencies. They can mess up the matching of our *I am.* Often an agent has worked with several other *I ams* and has a good working relationship and reputation.

The fetus comes through the birthing canal and enters the great forgetting. The child starts unfolding its awareness around two years old. It's no longer directly working with the first point of contact in the agency alone. The *I am* baby is settling into the new DNA skinsuit and is learning from the parents and the environment. As babies, we have full access to the vagus nerve which means we are still connected to the mystical side of this existence at a larger level.

The vagus nerve is like a control room. It operates the body with its special skills. The *I am* is housed in the vagus nerve with access to the entire consciousness of the DNA experience. As the *I am* gets older, it works with different levels of authority within the agency. Often at puberty the *I am* fires the existing agency. The *I am* says: *I have to be a sovereign being in this lifetime and as such, I need to take back my sovereignty from all these I ams represented by the agencies.* Most of it happens subconsciously. The level of hormones drives us during puberty. The *I am* apex presence here and now has the power to boot out other *I ams* if they are trying to run the agenda through the *I am* apex by corrupt agencies or soul families. Agencies can also be shared by soul families.

A bankrupt *I am* is someone who gave up the responsibility of creating their reality. They handed over authority to the programs and former *I ams.* It could be a person in a post-life review who chose not to cross over right away and hung around as a temporary ghost. This creates a longer form of shadowing and fractured soul shards. When finally crossing over the *I am* no longer has a point of contact to assist with the life review and future fetus planning. There are times when a living person has become a bankrupt *I am* or has given all authority away.

The *I am* apex has the power to out-create itself. An *I am* at any point can go into the vagus nerve and begin the journey of self-mastery, self-healing, self-nurturing, and kick out the negative programs that are in there. There are times when we give authority to a protective part of us, a program, a self-created demon. It takes authority. It says, *I get to work with the agencies you don't*. It does not give us any indication, no memo or email.

When bad things happen in our lives we are usually not in our *I am*. We're not fully in our body and vagus nerve. We're not in the driver's seat. False synchronicities can be created when an *I am* has too many soul shards in them. The soul shards begin to take over the *I am* spot in the vagus nerve. They contract with the actual agency in unawareness of the *I am* that has made the original contracts. To step back into the mighty *I am* apex takes daily practice.

Agencies can work in multiple time-space equations. Agents inside the agency are certified to work in time and no time. Some agents work with other non-certified agents of other time-space equations to force a match no matter how minute it is. Agents and the agency are separate entities. Think of them as independent contractors who are contracted by an agency to do the work. Some agents are full-time employees and some are outsourced contractors, akin to when a bank sells a product and bets against what they're selling you. Even though the *karmic resolution machine* has run its course, we as beings are still attempting to reincorporate our fractured selves, our traumatized and charged perspectives. This allows the agencies to use those traumatic experiences as a perspective for matching us to let go of karma and work towards dharma.

The agencies contracted out in the womb are still working with us in the now, but as long as domination and control still exist, where we are forced to accept tens of millions of layers seen and unseen, we will be dealing with agencies and contracted agents of agencies who have three degrees of separation from the responsibility for the destruction they cause. The *I ams* working against us can be resolved with contract revocations, shamanic work, and the daily practice of self-mastery. We all have parts of us that work for the domination and control agency. We have *I ams* that work for thousands of different agencies throughout the universe. High-level shamanic work is getting rid of the one-star agencies to only start working with the five-star agencies. Low-level agencies have a very low standard of a signature frequency match. Higher quality agencies have higher standards of match-making. The agency is here to help you write a contract on the fly. That is the best resolution for all sides. Low-level agencies look for lower levels of resolution to get their quota.

The vagus nerve is the universe in realized potential. The *I am* must learn to drive the vagus nerve like a race car driver. The Schumann resonance is the speed limit. The agencies like to give us speeding tickets without authority to slow us down. There are construction zones where the *I am* sets up a building phase and at times the *I am* creates a rebel who screws up the plans. This is when traumas take over life planning. The fetus gets shut out of this part and tries to get itself back into trust with the *I am*. These are the blame, shame, guilt, and fear agents that exponentially get worse with age. Faith is a key component to understanding the levels of separation.

Loss of faith and trust is loss of control of the vagus nerve. Once we lose control of the vagus nerve we are in a self-made crisis ruled by hesitation and doubt. When there is no coherence between mind-heart-spirit, there cannot be a resonance to the seen and unseen world that is trying to align synchronicities to us without us being paranoid about them. We start attracting low-quality agencies and the Schumann resonance is there to determine how powerful and potent we can be throughout an era or slice of history. It is only the agencies, or self-created internal programs, that put out the speed limit signs. The highway goes in every direction but we still have to guide ourselves with confidence from point A to point B, which is the resolution of conscious awareness at the level of responsibility as an *I am* of someone who is fully realized in the vagus nerve on the superhighway of the self. The speed limits can be seen as programs that need to be taken out or considered as data and input to learn and evolve. Conspiracy theory is an example of speed limits to slow us down. The system of domination and control is a low-level agency. Agencies have different levels of practices and standards.

Let's say we want to go into spirituality and not do the nine to five work life. We deliberately put in a construction zone to limit the speed of any programs that may want to take us off that path. It is how the *I am* sets up the discipline of the self. Many spiritual paths say our lives are written before we are born. It's true. They are *outlined*. Our free will decisions inform the outcome of the blueprint. In classical Greek thought, we have the notion of fate and destiny, a reiteration of the eastern adage of the life outlined before birth.

Our journey to self-illuminated master means we can't let our programs influence us to make hasty choices that don't work in our long-term favor. Programs bring up a subject matter. They have charge and polarity behind them. When we give into them the program in the vagus nerve is running us and not the *I am*. The planned construction zones are all about frequency, vibration, and harmony. They aren't necessarily a bad thing. They're here to help us on the path. There are deconstruction zones where a person has had lifelong trauma and needs to stop the traffic, completely tear up the roads, and create a detour so there's only one new neural pathway from which to choose.

Agencies will look for how present we are so they can match us with a being of similar resonance to our time-space equation. This is what we can call time syncing. Once you are in time sync with an agency it can contract for you — people, places, things, objects, art pieces, anything that can create an experience that manifests a memory with lasting expressions. Astrology has a big part in how the agencies can work with us. It builds on what sticks in light memory or trauma memory and from there a blueprint is formed. The system of domination looks to predict us the same way and tries to get us to work with its corrupt agency.

A spiritual strategy is an agenda in your time-space equation so that things can naturally time sync with you and you are not forcing them. Often people can't find their perfect mate because they are trying to force matches. It's a pure energetic thing that does not have a cognitive function behind it. The purpose of the *I am* is to make conscious things in a time-space vocation, to have access to its vagus nerve, equal to its level of awareness so a series of experiences can transcend chemical memories. Those chemical memories become powerful light memories that allow us to remember things about us during the great awakening, part of the ascension into higher states of being while still present in this world.

The agencies in the world are no different. They're expressions of the universal principle of agency, a third party facilitating an exchange between two or more parties. Madison Avenue and the age of advertising brought the agency to full expression. Our society needed to reach a point of complicated interdependence before fully formed agencies could appear and have such force and sway in the world. The advertising agencies create demand, which requires supply, which demands borrowing, which catalyzes money issuance, which expands the economy, which appears to validate the whole process. Man-made agencies are very destructive for the most part. Money itself is an agency, but that's not the limit of its magic. It's also its hyper-exchange. It never stays in position very long. It's even being offered a digital corpus now, a true form and world to exist within.

The other big area of the agency is public relations. That's why famous and busy people have press agents. Public relations is the agency that edits the global narrative. It's not that they lie; it's that they choose which questions to ask and which questions to answer. Without publicity, nothing happens big. So public relations is geared to making the biggest noise in the most controlled way. These are the absolute masters of complicated context and detail configuration for narrative support. We might never catch them in an outright lie, but their failure to live the law of truth makes them dubious agency for us because of how detached they are from the consequences of their actions. We can think of a dozen things in a second, the brilliant crafting of the Clinton defense — *I did not have sexual relations with that woman* – factually true within a self-defined context, and why? Because the person asking the question didn't clearly define sexual relations, so he used his own, then the blue dress blew away his self-defined context and brought it into communal context — he got his dick sucked in the Oval Office, and he doesn't consider it sexual relations because there was no penetration, and it only took several weeks and millions of taxpayer dollars to arrive at that stunning conclusion, all televised on CSPAN, like some funky mix of the Roman Coliseum and a Colombian daytime soap opera. The manifest agencies are here for the global narrative. It's their system. It creates its agencies, and those are their agencies. It's possible to push this understanding into the other dimensions and very easily understand what bad agency means in brokering a life.

The last form of agency worth noting is the agent assigned to you by the state for a legal defense. In bail court, this might be a low-level public defender. If the charge is more intense, say murder, then you might pull a defense lawyer with some clout, someone from a private firm who takes the public defender wage contract and acts as your lawyer. This is a dire form of system agency and mandated by the system itself because it knows you can not survive without an agent from their conceptual world, their jurisdiction. This is the world of agencies, here on the earth, and in the other dimensions, too, operating under the universal principle of agency for the resolution of contracts in the world and karma imprinted into the sound and light hologram throughout ancient past, immediate present, and the unrealized future.

Entangled and Unentangled

As we move past a subject, part of our brain continues to color in the past event, as if it were a live memory, until we completely disentangle from the subject. We do it all the time, so much we don't even notice we're doing it. We go to a party. We have a good time. We synchronize with the moment. Upon leaving, the energy of the party persists in us with a kind of half-life — still thinking and feeling the fun we had at the party and *coloring* the memory until our consciousness disentangles from the energetic imprint.

We want to stay with high-frequency experiences, but we get disconnected. Sleep can disconnect us. An argument with a significant other can alter our frequency, but, even a few hours after the argument, it was still a fun party. Think of a kite and the wind that suddenly reconnects to the energy.

Our state of perception influences us. When we *think back on* the party we are in the *implicate, enfolded order,* as opposed to being *at the party,* where we are in the *explicate, unfolded order.* The state of perception — implicate or explicate – determines how we perceive the physics of the environment. The physics of the environment, as well as the observer's perception, changes as the observer moves between explicate to implicate order. The state of perception equals perspective. The perspective of the explicate order — when we are at the party — is different than the perspective of the implicate, the memory. No matter if we are spiritual, atheistic, or anything else, it's all quantum mechanics expressed in different words.

The entangled observer uses a deeper information process, while, with the unentangled observer, the information is in full flow, and there is no need to process it — it's already in their knowing. When we have infinite love co-creating with us, we must truly choose to be the disentangled observer. Go into your heart space. Create that vision in your mind and engage with the sacred, neutral observer, knowing information cannot change us unless we agree to it. Based on how the *I am* now is understood and processed, it will either expand or contract your knowing. By making that sovereign choice to be the disentangled observer of the self means we get the fullest versions of ourselves in the here and now. You are the apex of your hierarchical order. Say that in your mental heart space — *I am the apex of my hierarchical order and no other hierarchical system has control and domination within me.*

The entangled observer, going through the process of perception and perspective, is refining the thought structures. Every time we have an *aha* moment we go from implicate to explicate. You can be an implicate unentangled observer and be in the explicate observation simultaneously, but entanglement is a deeper choice to enter into it.

In this reality, there are no real truths and facts because every time we go from implicate to explicate and back the memory has changed. This is what shatters space-time as the foundation of everything and creates the plasticity of reality. Consciousness does not adhere to space-time per the rules of Newtonian physics. Why would it? Consciousness is not of matter, but it can exist within and experience matter. We've been over this. You are a supernatural being who stopped being super and has been convinced it's not beneficial to the natural world. Did you get that? They're telling you you're preternatural, which is disconnected from the supernatural implicate and the natural explicate. They are trying to write us out of creation, void our contract with creation, erase us from time by convincing us we should never have occurred. It's random, don't you know, this evolution thing, this natural selection thing. A random thing has no plan, no order, but not to worry, from that chaos they can bring order.

Thoughts and memories, even as part of the implicate and explicate order, are a chemical frequency in nature. There comes a point in light frequencies where we bypass the chemical frequency in nature, and we operate in a higher dimension where space and time are no longer relevant. This is the temporality of time, the impermanence of it. Space-time is dependent on how the implicate and explicate order goes to chemical and light memory storage long term. This is when the DNA instrument of experience can have a three hundred and sixty degree view of itself. Spiritual contracts can become part of the implicate and explicate order. This creates the time stamp on the linear side of the life form, or, the DNA instrument of experience. It also creates adherence to the global narrative. The past, present, and future are irrelevant based on perception, but it is the perception that gives it relevance at the moment when the chemical memory becomes a light memory or, in the case of high frequency, when we bypass chemical memories to create an experience. The status of entanglement determines the outcome. Quantum physics works on the premise that everything is entangled. It places all significance on the observer without looking at the observer status of entanglement.

An unentangled observer may be implicate and explicate at the same time. You don't have to have an explicate explanation as a prerequisite to the implicate order. Every time the quantum field is accessed and observed, the access and observation creates a marker point in time and no-time that the implicate and explicate order is no longer defined separately but viewed simultaneously. We can call back all marker points in time to which you are a fixed point in space-time for spiritual resolution.

When we become a fixed moment in space-time all of our simultaneously existing selves can tune into our finite point in time. Those particular marker points in time could be many eras of light apart, or they could represent a marker point in an era of light in which we became an apex of our DNA lineage of registry. You could liken it to puberty — that would be a marker point in time. The era of innocence ends. The adult with miles to go before it sleeps, and promises to keep, to borrow from Robert Frost, emerges. It's a marker point in time because a greater form of time stamping is created. Sound is a form of light. Light makes up memories. Memories can be changed. Yes — memories can change. We can change our memories. We can change our past. This is the power given to every one of us, but few access it in a lifetime. It's just another forgotten part of the grand being we call soul.

The study of mnemonics is incorrect. Scientists understand the chemical part of memory, but not the light part. Past, present, or future memories are all frequencies of light. When we watch a video it is a slice of time. When we create a document or read out loud with power, these are slices of time.

This is what these revocations are for and if you read them from the heart, from a place of power, expanding the wholeness that is you, bringing the fullness of your sacred discipline, your sacred genius to mean what you say. Read them out loud as often as you can. Once you have found the power in your voice, record them. Listen in a deep meditative state. Hear your version of power. Present your signature frequency to that past incarnation of you and raise that frequency, that emanation of light, through sacred discipline and choice. These are choice points, markers in time. They project to a future version of yourself who may not be in that power or ready to get to the next level.

Introduce yourself to yourself with this method and you begin to learn you are your greatest teacher, you are a signature frequency match for what you focus on. You are a match for great change when it has potent concepts behind it that directly connect to you. By way of these tools, powerfully applied in the physical present moment, we make a conscious choice to be the unentangled observer, to interpret more data and data sets at a superluminal thinking level, enforcing our sovereignty as divine co-creative celestial beings of the now.

The unentangled observer is not attached to information or its flow. Until we become the unentangled observer, we impact situations purely through observation. We create another neutral observer external to us after this. We create it inside the divine hologram. We raise our light frequency to create that anima part, reaching towards the celestial medium journey, increasing our frequency until we are the celestial medium. This hasn't manifested in the human information field yet. Nobody in science or spirituality is talking about it.

One might very easily have questions about judgment here. How do you participate in family, community, economy, government, and world affairs as an unentangled observer? Suspend judgment. Judgment is an attachment to this divine hologram we are born into. It's also a petition for experience. This is our unconscious understanding of irony. To detach we need to practice the unentangled observer. We can achieve a non-judgmental state, non-competition, equal co-creation, with non-hierarchical order. It is our natural state.

Judgment is a very unique perspective. There are certain high states of awareness that use judgment. Judgment is an ongoing challenge all consciousness is going through. Making something absolute is necessary to solidify concepts, but it can prevent greater states of awareness. Judgment is required to materialize concepts from the sea of consciousness. This is another way of looking at materialism. It's not all just cash and cupidity. Certain highly aware beings are very judgmental. They've gone so far into concepts of good or bad it's their way or no way.

An unentangled observer can observe the quantum field without affecting it. It happens all the time. Observers are born into human form, sent into this world to create a record of it they then take back to where they came from. They do not interfere with the unfoldment of circumstance here. If they did, they would be entangled. There are numerous observers and collectives of observers that we might call off-world, able to observe us nonetheless. They are not influencing us, but they have a perception of us based on the observed data that is put back into their form of experience — their body if you will, like the human form for us — or what we can call, however *clinical,* the DNA instrument. The experience is taken in as a flow, then perceived after the time of observation. This allows them to remain unentangled observers because they are two degrees of separation from the original observance. The DNA does not influence the observation because of the two degrees of observation from the observed. It is our birthright and legacy as human beings to do that too. The more degrees of separation the easier it is to become a quantum observer. As we unentangle ourselves from everything that will give us the choice to perceive from a place of non-definition. DNA has a light frequency in it beyond our understanding. Our consciousness can engage the unseen world and by using mystical linguistics our knowing can expand. As an unentangled observer, no charge, no polarity can influence us. You have the unlimited point of view, in sacred neutrality where all information flows as an experience in expansion of your knowledge. This is when the mystical becomes the norm.

Near Death

Near Death Experience (NDE) is an excellent way to illustrate the light versus the chemical realities. It's a living example of a middling experience between chemical and light memory. They are part of the spiritual contract to allow us to see who, what, and where we've been in the lifetime since our first breath. It might also be our past and future lives intersecting. We often meet our guides, guardians, and others in the NDE.

The body has to go through the trauma of the death ritual. The aura somewhat pops and the contained life force starts leaving the body. After the pop, there's a vacuum of energy. The body must produce more etheric — chi, prana, orgone, to name a few monikers it goes by – energy and maintains it to stay alive. The final breaths use the body's last alchemical fuel it's had from birth. The brain loses the interconnectivity with the organs. The organs remain a part of the divine hologram. The *I am* begins to disintegrate its structure. We go back to the ocean of awareness. We may have attachments to who we have been in previous lifetimes. This triggers life reviews and direct healing of the body. We connect back into the original blueprint of health. Some people have visions of places and spaces of potential to refill the soul's capacity. Going through this transcendence phase, it's vital to maintain the auric bubble around ourselves. If not we drain out our life force energy.

We can come back from an NDE as an educated, illuminated being. Some people come back with abilities they didn't have before, the ability to play the piano, for example. It's a change in spiritual contract underwriting the incarnation — a new set of DNA-based purposes. This is not a walk-in experience. Walk-ins are extremely rare and often get misidentified with NDEs.

NDE experiences take us out of time-space equations because we move into the ocean of awareness then back to our life. Once we lose connection to the organs, it's just the vagus nerve and the spinal column reporting data the body has gone through. We are disconnected from the hologram because we are no longer supported by the aura. You can't maintain the internal energy flow. It flows out of the body. Once we lose the bubble around us we are no longer in the shared reality rules. We waver between many different worlds, including the ocean of awareness as our ancestral connection. The sea of consciousness is more for the many dreamers traveling back and forth, contracted with us on linear and non-linear scales to ensure we stay invested in an era of light and don't check out before our time.

As we leave time and space, depending on the kind of NDE we have, we can go to a high-density dimensional realm. This is when the fetus in the womb had a grand goal not yet achieved. We can be sent to seventh or eighth density to experience life from there then return with some of those potent memories intact. Often people are overwhelmed by the experience. They are overwhelmed by their light being. It becomes an expression of their self they fear they can not live up to. We can live the light body. It's already who we are. The NDE shows us that. Those experiences are contracted out in the fetus womb plan.

Bystanders sometimes accompany the soul when meeting loved ones on the other side. Life reviews can be seen as random moments, even though everything has an underlying universal order. When one has a life review as part of their NDE, it is about the spiritual contracts, help to grow beyond them because the soul, in the internal and external infrastructure, hasn't been able to resolve the issues. The fetus in the womb plans all sets of experiences, including the NDE.

When doctors or nurses or family members perceive light leaving the body it can be the etheric, the life force leaving the body at the end of the transition process. This is a verifiable phenomenon. The energy has a light mass. The body is twenty to twenty-two grams lighter after death.

It all depends on how the life and death experience is planned in the fetus. Some people have mystical deaths. These deaths are another way of assisting others to mend broken faith.

Out of Body Experience (OBE) is generally astral travel. This is markedly different than an NDE. The astral body has an intact auric bubble to store chi within the hologram. In a life review, the *I am* perceives incidents from all different angles because of the dissipated life force. The life force in the incarnation is the foundation of the *I am.* We may experience the pain we've inflicted on others as if being in their bodies. It can be quite dramatic. Many experiencers report an array of thoughts. Thoughts have an electrochemical frequency employing the body's base electromagnetic frequency as a storage system. This is how we create time stamps. In near death experiences, the body releases those energies. This is why the thoughts come to our awareness. An infinite being in the ocean of awareness can still experience these feelings as part of death.

Physical reactions help us acknowledge and resolve experiences once we return from the NDE. As the body takes the last breaths, a chemical reaction persists for as many as seven days. This is attachment. The death process can be dragged out in letting go of these attachments. In many mourning rituals, the bereaved stay with the dead body to honor and witness the letting go of all the karma and dharma as an alchemical form of resolution for the deceased and the bereaved.

The life review is part of the transition process and cannot be bypassed. We all must do it. On the verge of death, we don't necessarily remember what to do. Some people understand death as part of the journey and have prepared for it. Some people are in fear and panic over death. Our guides and guardians assist us to begin the life review regardless. Sometimes things we have deliberately avoided our whole lives come into focus. An understanding of the preciousness of life is recognized in the dwindling of consciousness.

Death is a new beginning. It's a change of energy and consciousness. Don't be afraid of it. Our choices in this life determine the ease we have with our life review. The understanding of death expands consciousness and takes away fear. Death is an acceptance to ensure that you have lived your life without regrets.

We don't necessarily have all the higher levels of awareness available when going through a life review. When the life review starts, the soul is shattered into thousands of shards. The oversoul comes in and puts them back together, takes out the negative soul shards, and puts them into a secondary file. Another fetus from another womb uses the soul shards to integrate it into the infinite fetus blueprint choice so the shards can get resolution in another lifetime. Soul shards are not the *I am*. The oversoul guides lifetime after lifetime.

The Literal Metaphor

Observation is also implicate order awareness. The observer effect should not have come so early in the crystallization process. Some people can have a three sense observation and still access the ocean of awareness — another bloodline influence example. Free will is tainted by the bloodline. We grow additional strands of awareness. The ocean of awareness and the sea of consciousness crystallizes and changes the bloodline at a certain level of acceptance and integration. This is the journey of the celestial medium — *I transfer the allness of myself to become the celestial medium. I no longer need to grow in this narrative. The next narrative I grow is in the spiritual commerce network.*

We are hypothetical beings. We can believe in many things. The universe determines what manifests through our wills. Hypothetical becomes *I am*. It's realized through engaging our belief engines which allow strands of awareness to influence intuition — precognition and post cognition — without competition or hierarchy. A multidimensional being manifests into this third dimension through created tangible experiences co-created with the infinite celestial medium. The incarnate life form is the expression of the present, the here, the now.

Epigenetic urges influenced by memories often keep us from creating new experiences. We have lived billions of incarnations. We must disconnect from them and reconnect with the source. This is the way to create new memories, which is part of the awakening journey. We sometimes over-identify with aspects of our evolution. Identity as myth is rarely explored, but it can hugely influence the way we experience life, and how we create in it. The more we identify with one part of our journey – grand earthly masters of manifestation or spiritual celestial mediums – the more we limit ourselves and inhibit our access to the possibilities of the many divine holograms. Buckminster Fuller immortalized the phrase — *I seem to be a verb* — when it came to considering identity.

> I live on earth at present, and I don't know what I am. I know that I am not a category. I am not a thing — a noun. I seem to be a verb, an evolutionary process — an integral function of the universe.

Identity is a strange thing. Thought is not static, it's a process of movement. Different metaphors in our belief engines change the very nature of the internal representation. By looking at celestial mediumship from this different perspective, we can change the way we identify with it, gain clarity and ease on how we interact and work with it. Ask — *what does celestial mediumship look like for me*: a ship that helps us sail through the ocean of awareness and the sea of consciousness, a vehicle we sit behind, a building we construct? It's all about the unique way we internalize the subject matter to fractalize the strands of information, enter it into cognition, and realize it in the here and now. Talk in pictures. A metaphor may be alchemically internalized as an expression of a multidimensional, multifunctional being of photonic light.

The theories with which astronomers and scientists explain the origins of the universe are bunk. Most hallowed information in the public space is disjointed. We might get the right details in the wrong context, the wrong context with the right details, or any number of percentages of either. Deception is a long practiced craft on this planet. It's a dividend of the great forgetting, the disconnection from source initiated by our birth on this planet. These deceptions, largely centered around information anemia — plus a host of techniques to lower our frequency — create and sustain belief engines. This has fractured the unity between cosmology, science, and spirituality. They don't want a unified knowledge system. Knowledge is licensed and sold back to us. It's a slave economy, but the belief engines inhibit this realization.

To understand the complexity of creation, a unified view of the holographic nature of reality is required. This exists outside the linear and beyond scientific sets of equations. We first need to understand time. Time and the nature of reality as a holographic system that evolves adapts, changes content and rules, and simultaneously updates events in the past, present, and future. Time is a social agreement — a paradox with different timelines, time genocide, creational and non-creational events — and, as such, the history we know it is incomplete, falsified, and subject to change in the years to come.

We need to look at time from the bigger perspective. The consciousness of our sun continuously expands. It's the total sine-wave of consciousness that represents our solar system, and it's spiraling around the galactic central sun. This means we can go a little faster. Time gets redefined at this point because our concept of time is very distorted. A time frame stated in a book is not a reliable reference. Time does not work linearly. History changes depending on what timeline we're observing. Time is a social agreement. How many calendars do we have in this world? We entangle with many variations of time: universal time, Greenwich Mean Time, Daylight-Savings Time. Time is no longer a universal concept. When we look at events in the past we need to take time travel, timeline genocide, and hijacking of events by time interference into consideration. The time wars have been centered on power, control, and dominance.

Language

The DNA skinsuit converts light into sound through consciousness to create memories. We perceive, receive, interpret, store, and express ourselves in words as codes, multidimensional patterns we call language. We may know multiple languages, speak in one language but process and think in another until we become fluent. A skilled linguist can speak seven or eight languages and easily switch between them. Language is a form of communication, consciousness being expressed verbally, emotionally, and physically.

The written word is light information stored in ink. It may take hundreds of thousands of years for the data to be perceived as light again. Language is a choice beyond cognition. It is the currency — a current energy voltage going through us. It is a medium to express ourselves. Sometimes many currents are going back and forth, an opera, for example, singing and dancing to accentuate, punctuate, and make the language more robust.

We think in perfect sentences. Nobody remembers learning to speak their first language, their mother tongue. We struggled to find the perfect sentence, but it all made sense in our heads. The light that is the pureness of our consciousness knows what it's trying to say, and it translates from light to sound. Syntax and sense can be independent of each other — *colorless green ideas sleep furiously*. It does not have to make sense to feel good. A word is not a creation. A sound is. The light can be modified with intonation to create more light. Martin Luther King said, *I have a dream*. Out of context, it's superfluous. In the context of a unified world, it allows the actual intonation process to create flashes of light. They create more flashes of light.

We can create light with our speech. Grammar is sentences flowing together to create a sensation, the breaking up and assembling of the words, the nouns, the pronouns, so we understand the mathematics of creating a sentence in English at that particular time. That alone does not make you a good talker or writer. You still have to be able to authentically emanate the words.

It's more like the nature of teaching. Language is spatial awareness. Grammar and syntax are the way consciousness adds intuitive wisdom to the statements themselves. It adds more to the code. When you look at words as sound waveforms we can see patterns like DNA intertwinement. We exchange DNA light at a higher perspective level. DNA changes through observation, the interaction between different types of consciousness. Everyone allows a different layer of change. Words are powerful. Incantations are words. Prayers are words. Mantras are sounds.

Certain phrases can put a shock into a person's system. Words can place us on the path of understanding or cast us out to outer darkness. Mythology is the potency of language memorialized. All the ancient myths were oral. The storytelling was the entire bureaucracy of the tribe, preserved and performed by shamans with the full authenticity of their voices. Joseph Campbell unpacked these myths to form vast maps of the unconscious. He distilled them all down to the hero, the central myth of all cultures. The hero is a light bringer. The light is new knowledge. The bringer of fire, the means to reproduce fire at will, was a hero in his time. They told stories about him for generations. Fire was a big deal. The story of the fire starter carried his light forward for generations as people huddled around fires at night.

Language has its consciousness. Children are in a learning state as they grow. They are exploring words, places, positions. They have focus and a strategy as they understand placement, position, and timing. If we hit an annunciation perfectly it creates a euphoric feeling within us. There's an actual dopamine journey behind owning that fluent form. Where there are no barriers, the language becomes instinct and pattern recognition.

A child is listening long before they are speaking. There are subsections within language. A thought in a conversation is fluid. We don't know what we're going to say next, but we have an intention when we continue a conversation. It maintains a conscious state of focus to continuously translate light into sound. It creates a lasting memory so we can understand the nature of our conversation. Thoughts can be stimulated by words. A new language is a mathematical journey of structure. Mastering the body's annunciation and conjugation journey by using intonation, the starting and stopping of the nasal process. There is a mathematical formula to mastering the tongue, nose, throat, and lips, and how the innate body language of each language affects the intonation journey.

It is an understanding of how fluent energy works together with all those pieces and parts. The inhalation of air from the lungs, the trachea, the larynx, the vocal cords, the force of the tongue, the nose manipulating the sounds to make intonation resonance with the lung. Certain words resonate from the lungs to the nose. The subtleties on how the wind forms in the lungs and is being used are intricate to the language. All of those mechanics make learning a new language difficult.

The tongue is the second organ that gets created. The heart is first. The tongue takes the vibration directly from the heart and sends it to the tip of the tongue so the heart's vibration is the base of our language. The tongue emanates an energy that we perceive in light. The position and placement of the tongue and teeth create a piezoelectric effect on the teeth, producing an electromagnetic effect in the body as unseen energy of expression. The roof of our mouth has three plates that determine how chi is spread through our bodies. If they are tight, with a sunken nasal passage, there's an occupying presence taking away from the greater us to express. The sinus along with those three plates creates a vibration that is our expression. The tongue works like Morse code, tapping and creating electromagnetic signals the brain receives as language. The heart sends the language through the tongue. The brain receives it. There are conversations in which we go beyond the five senses, into a holographic perception of the language suspended in our consciousness while we process it. Some people process faster than others. Slow processors understand the subject matter better in the long run. They don't allow themselves to be overwhelmed by the data or over-process, and they don't miss nuances.

Humans are analog speakers trying to achieve a dual process. We are analog and digital thinkers. Off-world species no longer operate in binary coding. They think from multiple perspectives. It allows them a greater understanding of the unlimited point of view. They are waiting for us to come out of the limitation our language imposes on us. The global narrative blocks language from evolving into multidimensional thinking. The entire body gets involved in communicating. Words make up the least significant part of our rapport, less than ten percent. The rest is expressed through our tone, tempo, timbre, volume, and physiology, as in posture, gesture, breathing, facial expressions, and blinking.

We often use hand positions when explaining dense material, using the streams of light in our hands to examine the field and the strands we want to connect with. It is like moving the sheets of information around to get to the specific data faster, a way of determining sub information and how that affects the whole. It is almost like we are using the hands to complete a spiritual process. When we speak light language it's through the throat chakra. All of our senses observe the vocal patterns the reality is observing through the throat chakra. The knowing is in the heart. The completeness of the manifestation is in the voice — the throat chakra. We are setting a tone and frequency.

People might not speak a language, but they can still intuit a body language, an auric field interacting with it, and the psychic information which is the sign form of light language. Speaking light language uses all parts of our body. The final manifestation is how the reality interprets it as an observer or an unentangled observer. Light language can speak to unentangled observers and be unentangled, yet it still gets the point across. We have the right to speak with them.

The *I am* presence is the apex of this hierarchical order. We can use our words of command to be in dominion or communion with beings. When our light bodies are calibrating more with the *I am* presence, languages through our soul and voice box become easier. The translation is free flowing with harmony in which several phrases before you speak light language can get changed and modified, the expression of photonic light. We are giving codes to light itself to change an expression, like a kaleidoscope opening and closing a specific pattern. We can make multiple sets and patterns throughout the entire conversation. It's almost like we remember how to use the frequencies of the voice intonations to affect reality. Every communication is multidimensional. An expansive communication is based on the broadcaster and the receiver looking at the match of the three-way forms of interaction of frequency, vibration, and harmony. When we speak a multitude of beings in the past, the future, the seen, and the unseen are listening. A high-frequency statement is low in harmony. It creates powerful sparks, not necessarily in the now, but later, for the people listening in archives and beyond.

It should come as no surprise that the controllers are heavily invested in language as well. The main tool of human agencies — advertising, public relations, and law — is language. The false god system is held in place largely with language. It's highly charged emotional language the creates a susceptible state and then the ideological template is fitted into that opening.

Political language is highly legal, seeking to incite feelings without committing to hard promises. Slogans are big too — build back better, hope and change, make America great again — again, an example of inciting feeling without a clear working intent for the emotion. This is energy harvesting at a low level, national, provincial, and municipal. However, it is disclosed energy harvesting. The politician discloses the political goals and we have a choice to lend our energy or not.

We have to commit our energy to this world in some measure, no matter how much zealotry we see in renunciate communities to the opposite. If you live in a group, you have to give part of your energy to that group. It's true for families, lineages, communities, states, countries, the world, the solar system, and the galaxy.

It becomes more about honesty, directness, lack of corruption, and sincerity, but the political class is bought before they even get to the office. Believe it or not, one of the things that will wake the most people up is the growing awareness of this corruption in our systems, and, most importantly, our language. It's not natural for human beings to lie. That's why we feel a little knot in the solar plexus when we lie. When this feeling goes away, and a person is so accustomed to lying it is their new normal, something vital is taken away from the person. They may finish their life, but they have created a karmic imbalance which has to be balanced. Language is a great gift, a disembodied spirit we all share. It should never be abused. All words spoken should be honest, from the heart and the tongue, and to affect your true purpose, which should be the best outcome for all parties as a result of the parlay.

Entities and Demons

A program may or may not be consciously entangled. It all depends on how life force empowered the program is. The more we are out of our body, letting the program run us, the more it's entangled with our vagus nerve. The vagus nerve gives it access to our special skills. It creates confusion about what is the soul and what is the program. Some people's bodies are controlled and run by programs. They take over the vagus nerve. The *I am* is unaware. Once programs take over we are susceptible to entity association. Entities can take over the programs. Karma determines the growth and veracity of actions entities take when they take over programs. Entities might not know they're being run by karma. It is easy to get lost between what is internally created and what is external entities.

Ninety-nine percent of entities are self-created. One percent is bonafide haunting. Not everyone is meant to work with entities. There's an intuitive factor to knowing what to work with. If we don't have the intuitive factor built-in we should not be in that realm. It's curiosity learning. It happens when we let the programs run us. When we are curious about something we are not the neutral observer. Curiosity itself has a charge and polarity. We are controlling a subject matter. It's right at the edge of the unknown. The brain fills in the unknown before it's known. People want to know and are falsely drawn to it by paranoia. It's a vibration in them saying, *I need to know about entities so they don't invade me.* They might not have had any around for months, but the curiosity draws them.

There are certain forms of energy we might confuse as an entity. They're just shards of us. They initially were part of the story we created, then they turned into internal programs when the story was empowered by charge and polarity. Trauma can develop from a scary story. It doesn't affect us or turn into full-blown fear, anxiety, or paranoia. We can go back to the original story we over-created, see the tree of creation for what it is and release the trauma. A lot of people need help to get back to that source. Not everyone can do it on their own. Certain people with ancestral DNA switches turned on don't have the capacity for that self-inquiry.

There are times when the story is so strong the entity takes over the life force and the person finds it impossible to disentangle. As healers, we have to slow down. We shouldn't go beyond the match of our vibration. The house always wins. You never know what's next when people are possessed. We are the alpha entity, but self-defeating habit patterns make our potential a low match to high vibration. Getting out of shame, blame, and guilt is the beginning of the healing journey.

When we are speaking to someone run by an entity we usually talk to both. We speak to them and the entity simultaneously because the person is both an entangled and unentangled observer in that scenario. Make the entity come out to a conversational match so we can speak to it. The client can be a fully unentangled observer listening to you talking to the entity even though he or she is using her vocal cords to respond to its thoughts.

When people work with very low-quality agencies to create, they often use us as a signature frequency match to get others into their web. They find it difficult to be on their own or need instant gratification and constant validation for their ideas and creations. As a healer or teacher, we will see that a lot of people falsely match themselves with you. When we know it is a false match, we can use it to our advantage and not create karma. Depending on the power of our vibration, if potent enough, their alter ego has to retreat and their *I am* can feel the vibration. The altered ego is usually a chicken shit. When the *I am* has to defend its actions, it shows us how misaligned with its sovereignty it is. We have to maintain a high vibration not to let chaos define the keynotes.

Shattered shards of *I ams* are either bankrupt or fractalized *I ams* unauthorized to deal with an agency but still take on this responsibility without our authority. We all come across these forms during the healing and teaching journey. Take someone who has been sexually abused at a young age who uses an altered ego to protect themselves emotionally. Then they go through healing, and they no longer need that shard, or, they use chemical drugs and create more shards, demons, vigilantes falsely protecting them.

An external demon is a life force that has not crossed over. It maintains itself as a surface bound energy spirit, draining the life force from others. It cannot produce its light. It could be an *I am* that did not want to pass over, or an off-world being that could live thousands of years but lost its capacity to maintain a single body. Its *I am* can create new bodies temporarily, but the vibration of this world doesn't allow these bodies to stay in existence long. This is why it possesses other bodies.

An internal demon is the result of intense trauma. The story becomes so big that the character goes into the vagus nerve and the subconscious empowers it to be the potent being, then it becomes the dictator, tyrant, and abuser through addictions, self-defeating habits, and self-sabotaging mutilations. The person's internal demons try to dominate and control the external demons. External demons often run as internal demons can be very strong and destructive.

An implanted entity is a powerful demon that has thousands of ways of harvesting energies off us. They control many minion demons much younger under their hierarchy. It's well documented in CS Lewis's *The Screwtape Letters*. It will implant into you, and its job is to pretend to be your inner higher voice until you won't be able to distinguish what is your voice and what is the demon's voice.

An explanted entity is something that has been put inside you to create a signature frequency match and then purposely ripped out to create a drama. Once outside of you it still vibrates on your frequency, serving as a bait line to lead you down a track of false synchronicities to negative external sources.

Inculcated entities are advanced puppetry — you don't know who or what is pulling the strings — a very old external demon source with lines into thousands of minions feeding up the tree.

A clone has a spark of the person in it. The spark has a similar spiritual contract pattern to the original being. It's against sovereign free will rules to collect an entity's DNA and make a clone of it. Cloning against someone's free will creates a person that is dominated and controlled with little or no sovereignty. This would enable other sentients to take over the body at any point. The vast majority of the world's trade beings are genetically built with a suit for consciousness to broadcast from one planet to another. That suit can be inhabited for some time and then put into cold storage for later use, or they unmanifest the body, travel energetically to a planet and manifest a body there.

Running into a fully depressed person can be tiring. It's important to know when you speak to the person or a program, an internal demon. When the person is in the body, the programs are shut off. Sometimes external entities can still come in. There are people with powerful external or internal entities in them who are subjugated. We can hear it in their voice — how meek they are. There is no power in their voice.

Source Connection

Source connection is living in the light worlds, the worlds above the elemental and chemical, while grounded in the body, finite and infinite at the same time. We disconnect to contrast being connected. It's an aspect of the lesson here — disconnection to understand the connection. We see this fundamental duality of the divine hologram everywhere — the yin and yan of the Tao, Carl Jung's extraordinary work on duality and the shadow, the juxtaposition to the light. Not many voices have clearly articulated the disconnection teaching before. The thread of life goes everywhere in the universe, and that *thread* has a connectivity bandwidth exponentially beyond fiber optic, and yet we, this human race, underwent the sensation of disconnection from source as an experience. Realize what that means. We're like Chilean miners trapped in a collapsed coal mine. That's how the connected species in the sentience circus that is our galaxy see us, hardcore. As we have steadily moved into self-awareness as a species, propelled as we were by Gutenberg, the Western enlightenment, the Industrial Revolution, and, lest we forget, the iPhone, we have seen this disconnection in the collective mind. It rippled through with French Existentialism as chic twentieth-century philosophy, spurred on by the First World War, no doubt, the trauma of it, the horror of it all. One of the earliest portrait's of this dislocation would most certainly be Mister Kurtz, from Joseph Conrad's *Heart of Darkness*, the perfect literary tone struck for the twentieth century, published in 1899, a harbinger if ever there was one. We are here to experience disconnection from the source. Oneness has no meaning if we don't understand the disconnection journey first.

The disconnection fractal is achieved by controlling the mind. People don't take a moment to realize the enormous changes the human race has gone through since about 1890. We now live in a completely man-made reality. We travel in an enclosed environment propelled by a tar plumbed from the earth. We have face-to-face conversations a thousand miles apart. We can drive past digital billboards in city thoroughfares. The Greek amphitheater is Netflix, HBO, and the cable channels. Stonehenge is Joel Olsen on a big sports screen, and the sacred is now profane. This is spiritual conquest. This is a disconnection from the source. Every artifact of our organic culture has been incorporated and sold back to us. Yet, by reasons only explainable through cultural or regional programming, we think it's unjust that Beijing select Catholic Archbishops instead of the Vatican, and reincarnated Rinpoches instead of the Tibetans. Regional and provincial narratives are more and more folding into global ones. The global narrative teaches us false science, false time by galactic timekeeping, false history, and belief systems which long ago should have given way to tangible and productive wisdom and knowledge traditions. False light is a multidimensional technology commonly used here. This is the source of disconnection.

Superluminal thinking leapfrogs chemical experience as the basis of memory and consciousness. Let's look at it backward through photosynthesis. A plant eats light and excretes oxygen. Human beings live in a chemical experience until light enters consciousness. It's the reverse of plants. We consume elemental material here, calories, an inherently chemical process, aided by a long digestive tract, and we use this energy, the fuel for the human experience, an integral part of our chemical existence, to find the light in our consciousness. Creation in a dual pole, free will space can often be navigated by bookends, opposites, even irony as a conceptual understanding of the thesis, because the opposites form contrasts, and, in a light based divine hologram, without contrast we would not even discern the reality around us. You see your reality, your wife or husband, your dog, your car because the environment has light. The light finds pockets and reflections, and it finds places it can not go, and from its presence are all forms etched.

Superluminal operates beyond the zeros and ones of the sympathetic and parasympathetic systems. The vagus nerve is fully functional. All the chakras are open and interconnected through the central nervous system. They are part of the superluminal experience. The body adds the sensation that it can't process, but it knows it's the unentangled observer in superluminal thought. The body grounds us here, but the consciousness can go beyond the speed of light to tens of millions of places and spaces simultaneously and collect millions of unique experiences in one-millionth of a second and come back with it fully processed. Then we go out and do it again and again until our cup is filled. Superluminal thinking is more than we have learned, read, and studied. It's knowing going to the next level, the next apprehendable sphere of experience. It's subtle. We won't have conscious cognition of it. Everyone has experienced it. Our level of practice will determine how fast we can apprehend it. How is that possible? You're already there. You just don't know it. You are unconscious of it. The unconscious mind is connected to all knowledge. The conscious mind creates a manageable data flow so you can persist in the illusion of the third dimension. This is the basis of the Maya teachings in Buddhism. Illusion was perhaps the wrong word. It's more like a projection of light refracting through the atmosphere, the projection itself emanating from the source of all our realities, the place without sound or light that is neither dark nor silent, Kabir's riddle.

The sound and light is all sound and light, not just what can be experienced within the human sense ranges for hearing and sight. All these inner worlds and universes, if they are at all apprehendable, are sustained by sound and light. Anywhere these two persistent emanations of the prime creator are present we find contrasts and then forms and then realities. It's this simple.

Chapter 4

Timeline Errata

Fifty Million Years

We are a one hundred percent free-will universe. That's no small thing, but because we have nothing to compare it to, nothing to create a contrast so we might see the form and blessing of free will in its proper context, we don't understand it. Humanity has been given free will on earth and in the whole universe. It's not common. Most universes are not free will.

What is free will? Free will means we can set up our realities based on rules we create in the free-will universe. Rules agreed upon are rules to follow. The growth of consciousness in the awakening journey expands upon the understanding and blessing of free will. When we become the celestial medium, we see a world of people walking into walls and saying someone or something struck them. That's how badly free will and the inherent aggregated karma have blinded humanity. It's like watching people drive blindfolded at rush hour.

Earth had drama while it was being created. Drama is natural. It adds tension to our lives. We love drama. It turns out a lot of other beings out there do as well. It's like a little charge in us. Look at the mating rituals of humanity, pure drama. Contested courtship can get bloody, then, when we get what we wanted, we question whether we ever even really wanted it. One moment we're ready to kill for something, the next it's last year's birthday present, and we're already generating dramatic tension for our next acquisition, bored with what we have already fought to attain. We're like self-loathing gods, unsure of our jurisdiction or role here while we're alive.

People have an ego, even at the higher dimensions. It just functions differently. When karma reaches the point where a sentient species can reach out several galaxies beyond their home planet, we can create karmic pollution to newer planets, younger planets. Earth was a planet that brought good and bad pollution to thousands of worlds. At inception as a seventh-dimensional galactic seed planet, earth's purpose was to have chakras on its planet called wombs, like a woman's womb. Anyone who lived above the womb chakra would have their sentience influenced to create DNA wisdom.

Fifty-one million years ago, the earth had already been ripped out of its home galaxy. The original dark forces who invaded from a warring galaxy came here, saw the earth, and said, *that's the prize*. All these other little planets were nothing to them. They captured the earth by spiritual invasion. This happens at the astral level. The incarnation process is hijacked by astral beings who did not originate here, resonate with earth, or add anything beneficial. They were brought here to demoralize and degrade the earth. They outbred the people already here in the astral-physical earth by creating more corrupted souls. What ensued was political devastation, land devastation, and dramatic wars with other places. Finally, a core group of dark beings emerged who took over the chakra system and the unity consciousness drive of earth. They teleported earth against its will to the *other* galaxy.

The first teleportation greatly injured earth. She was near death. Earth cried out to the universe and beyond for help. Massive migrations from the seven universes came to earth. They outbred the dark forces, kicking them off, but they still had the first interlinking of the anchor societies here. When the earth began its healing process — the dinosaur age — sentience had been removed from the surface. It was brought into an ethereal realm so the surface could graduate. The surface we live on is the graduating timeline. If we're here to become a higher dimensional soul and enter function with earth, or go out and explore space with our consciousness, we have to be on the graduating timeline. Earth has three timelines — above, below, and center. Center is the graduating timeline.

At this point, earth kicked off its first defense campaign. We reinforced the energies of the earth. We knew the spiritual invasion was coming again. It was only a matter of when in the timeline. This began the first pyramids to amplify the consciousness of earth after being ripped out of its original galaxy. The pyramids were placed on the chakra points based on the crustal points. They enforced the ability for the local sentience to create local realities. They made a grid around the earth. Any entering entity was screened to determine if it could make spiritual contracts with earth sentience. At that point, the dark forces had spread to a few thousand other worlds. They became more practiced in dominating, controlling, and mastering less evolved species.

The dark ones discovered earth would go through very light, very dark, and very dense periods in its galactic rotation. The dense spots were the place, the time marker, where they could spiritually invade *en masse*, lower the consciousness of the surface people by influencing DNA, soul families, soul contracts, getting us at every stage of the game, ultimately to remove how we naturally lived with our planet. We were disconnected from our ability to communicate and commune with the source.

There are nine layers of pyramids. Earth has been moved twelve times, captured twelve times. There are nine layers of fortification in the astral world. There's no other planet in the universe or three other universes that has been fortified this much. We're in a situation where the dark ones captured earth four to five times, then the light forces recaptured her four to five times, and on like this, a galactic soap opera. We have arrived at a situation where the fortification grid and quarantine put in place by the good guys is now the hindrance. We're a race with amnesia and we're a race held hostage, preyed upon by entities that want to take the powerful people somewhere else by their own belief.

We're entering another one of those periods, a harvest period, so to speak, or ascension, as some circles call it. We're going out of a very dense part and going into a very light part. Of the sixty-six planets in our solar system, the vast majority are in the light part of space. Earth and Mars are stuck in the dense part, anchored by the low consciousness people here. They anchor us here.

Our solar system has many salvage species visiting due to the ample ship debris from past wars. Things don't decay in space. A million-year-old ship would still have many valuable commodities. There are fifty million years worth of treasure in our solar system. Many races who get lured in, even on the astral, end up attached to the intense drama and gravity here and get sucked into the incarnation process here. The near-endless drama of free will subverted and restored has been the history of earth for all these many years, the prize of this solar system, this galaxy, this universe, and other universes. Earth has always been a battleground, the ultimate gladiator coliseum in a warring universe.

The Fifteen

After the first fall of Lemuria, they rebuilt their society, and there was a second rise of Lemuria, but this time they had to become more offensive. They had to defend themselves and Lemuria. This was tens of millions of years ago in linear time in this three-dimensional hologram. Lemuria had very little choice. To close some of the dramatic karmic timelines out there they had to militarize. The timelines of domination and control had begun on earth. There was karma to balance. The Lemurians went out and defeated peoples and places affected by earlier earth interference. They recaptured worlds under domination and control. At that point, there were as many as two-hundred thousand worlds under domination and control. It had spread that quick.

The fifteen multidimensional beings were here on earth. They were not part of the original creation here. They were founder beings who returned here. It's a touchy subject because it tips over a lot of sacred cows. Most spiritual paths and religions on the planet have been the creation of the fifteen, either one of them, a group of them, or all of them. It would be almost impossible for an average human to distinguish between one of them and a god. Why they came here, a new and developing galaxy, with the earth as its main planet, is unknown. The events leading up to their being here happened someplace else, another universe.

It raises huge questions about the creation here in the Milky Way Galaxy and our universe. It also commences our galactic narrative under a flawed creation model. The prime creator made mistakes here. It's an extremely hard thing for a culture of humans who believe in an infallible god to digest. The prime creator made a mistake or allowed ingredients into the recipe that changed the flavor of the creation. No matter how we look at it, the infallible god narrative has to go away. Where does that leave us? In the best position anybody could be in. It leaves us in a mature, responsible understanding of the prime creator. It is growing and learning alongside us. Everything in the life matrix on this planet has a relationship with the prime creator because everything animated by the prime creator is an extension of the prime creator. The prime creator is us and we are the prime creator.

One of the practices of the fifteen multidimensional beings was to trick other races, other peoples, into invading earth — it's always been about the earth, our wondrous seventh-dimensional seed planet — and two-hundred thousand worlds meant a lot of souls to spiritually invade earth. Spiritual invasion is done by hacking or controlling the incarnation grid. It takes place on the astral plane. The people are brought here in their astral form to the earth astral, which is the astral world associated with the earth. We need to go back to the divine hologram for a moment. Each world is a hologram, a sound and light fractal with its jurisdiction. If we take the physical three-dimension reality we are incarnated into, the one that has you holding this book in your hands right now, we are unable to go to other planets, other solar systems, or other galaxies, at least not physically, those of us not in the secret space programs anyways. It's the same on the astral. There are smugglers, people traffickers, and slavers on the astral — as above so below. If it happens here it happens there. This is how deep the corruption in our system has been. Nobody has spoken these things aloud. None of the vaunted lineage paths in the east or the west have given this teaching. It has been prohibited until now. Those human beings who have known about what is going on here have been a part of it. If any of the spiritual teachings on this planet had told the truth they would have been wiped out, and many of them were in the past, the real past, not the glued together history we have now which is perhaps ten percent accurate and nothing more than an adjunct of the global narrative.

The fifteen wanted to water down, to dilute the soul force of the Lemurians. It had to be stopped at the source. That's what the spiritual invasion was about. It mirrors what is done on the borders of countries they want to culturally destroy. If a culture becomes a problem it gets destroyed, and one of the ways they do that is mass immigration. This is one of the reasons why Western Europe and North America are being inundated with the poorest of the poor. Think of the logistics of Africans walking to Europe, or Hondurans walking to the United States. How much food and water would be required to sustain fifty thousand people walking three thousand kilometers? The countries they are walking through are very poor as well. Where are the Mexicans getting the extra calories to feed all these people? Where do they sleep? Where do they go to the bathroom? Walking twelve hours a day it would take forty days to get from Honduras to Texas. If you walked twelve hours a day your feet would be destroyed in a week or less. Ask anyone who has been in the military about marching and how much instruction on foot care they're given.

Please do not confuse what is being said here with a lack of compassion. Everyone has the right to take whatever risk they need to take by the direction of their heart to make a better life for their children. This isn't about compassion. If it were, the US State Department would make the country a priority and improve the lives of people in that country. That would be the most expedient way to help the Honduran people, who have been the subject of corrupt government, US-backed coups, land theft from the peasants for transnational corporate farming, and a litany of other crimes and indignities. The migrations are a microcosmic version of what the fifteen did millions of years ago. Contemplate this level of warfare for a moment.

The Lemurians were multidimensional. They knew what was going on, and they set up defenses. Cities were built out of crystal upon earth chakra points. Three-hundred thousand powerful Lemurian seers would sit in these crystalline cities, remote view, remote experience, and remote attack another planet's sentience, or its species on the surface, killing everyone there. It was a grim business, and the Lemurians were not predisposed to war by natural creation and evolution on earth, but it was the only way to stop the incarnating soul invasion.

It gets even weirder. Some of the invading force was us, the lineage of the human race here now on earth. The migration patterns were both emigration and immigration — some people leaving and some people coming. Lemuria's first rise and fall had a dramatic effect, massive migration away, then massive migration back. This cycle repeated.

All these wars are never-ending. Once something was destroyed there would be retaliation, the swing of the pendulum, the karmic tempo for this free will experiment we call our universe. It could take a thousand or a million years for someone to rebuild. There are now some two-thousand three-hundred races out there who have war karma with earth. The same fifteen beings from the beginning, from another universe, were the ones lighting the fire of anger in other worlds, so they would build faster, recover faster, and attack harder.

At this time, the time of Lemuria's second rise, there were three who were sixth dimensional, two who were seventh-dimensional, six who were eighth-dimensional, and the remaining four were ninth-dimensional. The ninth-dimensional ones came in with the third generation of immigrants from other universes. There were only three galaxies in our universe when these beings migrated here. We can call them the galactic mafia because they're separate of light and dark, even though they're both light and dark at the same time, but they're not neutral. Their goal was to become new galactic prime creators in this galaxy, which already had a prime creator. They wanted to use earth as their base. Its original mission to seed-free will life allowed them to go from galaxy to galaxy in an attempt to become the prime creator in the universe.

When this universe was created, the sentience created a contract with our multiverse to say *I'm going to be a universe* to create consciousness, evolution, and expansion, and invite immigrants from other dimensions to experience *free will.* These fifteen beings wanted to limit the free will one galaxy at a time.

The fifteen got into this beautiful system of life on seventh-dimensional earth. They started their mission from within the earth incarnation system. As Lemuria built to its peak factions formed in it. We had spiritual factions, scientific factions, no-technology factions, high-technology factions, and many more. Society fractalized, much like we're seeing now throughout the West and other parts of the world. These factions began *the separation* which took earth from a seventh-dimensional status to a sixth. The earth lost a whole quotient of its exponential energy. The separation caused a mass exodus. Earth was left undefended. She was captured. That was the first fall of Lemuria. The multidimensional beings who were here orchestrated that capture.

The new beings that came to take over earth reanimated Lemuria with the leftover refugee population. They began a domination and control system. It's important to understand that domination is multidimensional. We can appear to be living unshackled on the earth, but the shackles are astral and mental through programs, vibrational degradation, and lack of protection from the higher dimensional beings who were here before the demotion to sixth-dimensional status. The controllers began an incarnation pattern to bring in more of the kinds of beings they wanted from the other worlds normalized to domination and control.

At this point, the *good guys* of the rest of the universe decided they had to do something. There was a huge debate among the ascended masters, the philosophers, and the wisdom and light councils participating. There's galactic sentience which created a war in another galaxy. That galactic sentience allowed it to come here. This is the first mistake of the prime creator of our galaxy. The galaxy we are in was not ready for war, was not set up for war. War came, nonetheless. Once the karma of war enters a species it's very difficult to get it out. Blood oaths and blood bonds carry throughout time and form the basis of future soul contracts. Anything can happen in a free-will universe, but even this twisted the rules to a proportion not conceived in the original design of the prime creator.

The fifteen beings had aspects of themselves in all the large families. If there's a family crest, it's been hijacked by spiritual contracts. This is guaranteed on earth. There were those here we didn't know about, outside the framework of the Royals and so on, ones who kept themselves secret, created mystery schools that have ten students every generation.

The light councils took forever to adjudicate. The conundrum was beyond the collective wisdom available at the time. In the meantime, many species took up war to defend themselves. It was natural. That created the first line of drama. War is so embedded in the human consciousness now it's difficult to refute Judge Holden, a central character in Cormac McCarthy's *Blood Meridian* when he says, *All other trades are contained in that of war.*

Mars is akin to earth in its fate with war. It had high technology and low spirituality in its beginning. It was a commerce center, but it turned commerce into a military-industrial complex. When Mars and earth began their first lines of drama, earth needed technology to support the defense and fortification process. That is how Mars and earth got interlinked before they got brought into this solar system. What is remarkable to note are the literal threads in mythology. Take this missive on Mars as the Roman God of War from the *Encyclopedia Britannica*:

> Mars, ancient Roman deity, in importance second only to Jupiter. Little is known of his original character, and that character (chiefly from the cult at Rome) is variously interpreted. It is clear that by historical times he had developed into a god of war; in Roman literature, he was the protector of Rome, a nation proud in war.

Earth went into this circumstance where timeline war became the norm. Around four-hundred and eighty to four-hundred and twenty thousand years ago all the two hundred primary *soul families*, the soul groupings of some two-thousand three-hundred different species, so there's only a slight difference in the soul families, but all of them were in competition to make earth *theirs*, and all of them had time travel technology, inter-dimensional vessels, and all of them had explored the universe. They were all in competition to make that *first species*. This is the basis of the time wars.

What the dark ones started so many ages ago echos through our reality today. The original design of this galaxy was continual evolution and graduation. This is the natural, organic process. The abuse of time technology for warfare corrupted the incarnation process. The cycle was broken. People could not graduate. They're stuck in reincarnating over and over with a brief respite on the astral plane before being sent right back. Atop this, there are whole migrations of souls not allowed to incarnate here, stuck in our astral world, unable to go back without a lifetime here. Our astral worlds are overflowing with all these things that are just stuck. This created all kinds of mayhem, nasty entities in a very impatient mood in the earth astral space, easily passable for what we describe as demons in some scriptures. The entire system was blocked, with no graduations and no new classes.

After Lemuria went through its first fall and rise — some thirty million years ago — there was a period of stability, but the fifteen multidimensional were still here, plotting and scheming to usurp the galactic prime creator. Earth's entire history has been war and domination since the first fall of Lemuria.

The Lemurians were moving through time with their air cities. They had to assay each time earth was teleported. The old timeline wars ended because the x-y axis of the planet no longer provided a time baseline. The sentience that was part of the old timeline was still on earth, and earth adopted the sentience as the new *first species*. Those new first species became part of the Lemurian society and left with the Lemurians. They migrated away and became part of the drama and tension polluted reality out there and were forced back to earth. Earth has been very similar to baby-boom parents who have millennial children who leave and return home to live, an endless coming and going.

Lemuria tried to push out as many of the negative incarnating souls as possible. They were coming from seven thousand worlds under domination and control. It's no different than a country having a rush of immigrants. It's one of the ways the negatives have tried to dominate the worlds. The Lemurians did a great job. Negatives did get into the earth's incarnational cycle, but not as many as hoped for by the negatives.

As a result of the time wars and all the other mischief here, there has been no graduation — the movement of souls matured here to new experiential dimensions — for many cycles. The normal cycle is a lot like our education system. We go through a course of learning here and move on. Our curriculum is measured in eras of light and incarnations. Everything is interlinked and connected. When graduation doesn't happen here, other beings in our universe are held back from moving to their next level. The situation got like a Los Angeles traffic jam on a Friday afternoon, but the Friday lasted several eras of light. This is what garnered the attention of governing forces.

The prime creator is like a mafia boss. He sets up the new rules. The system activates around the rule parameters. Numerous classes of co-creators build out on the rules. The prime creator waits for co-creators to go against the rules — betray him. He doesn't need to know every move of the soldiers on the street. He's the boss. The co-creators are beings like us, *I am* instances of various planets and systems in various densities. The higher density co-creators can see everything below. They have the advantage of greater perspective. There's a catch. The co-creators could not create if they didn't have the prime creator as an aspect of their being. This gets tricky. There are many ways to explain it metaphorically or allegorically, which is usually the way it is done in creation stories, but the time has arrived for a more literal definition. The prime creator can only be objectified by a subjective experience, a mystical experience. Why? Because the prime creator is everything, including the co-creators. Therefore, if you reason it through, the prime creator has to be good and bad to balance the ever-present corruption. Corruption can be corrupted. You have to be the antithesis of it, the opposite of corruption — honest, transparent, sharing, good.

The prime creator's audit took place on March twenty to the twenty-second of 2013, the prime creator of this galaxy came in and audited this world's soul contracts from bottom to top — anything that's ever lived here, anything that's ever been stuck here — all of earth's soul contracts were read in a complete and total expression, so it came down to the final equation of where the earth was as it had traveled from the beginning of the setup of the management system we have now, the management system being *The Council of Twelve* – four light members, four dark, and four neutral. The neutral got kicked out by the dark ones. They said, *We'll kill ten billion of your people unless you leave.* The neutral contingent departed by compassion. The council reformed to seven light beings and five dark, meaning the dark could incarnate more of their lower-consciousness beings here, which would take earth's consciousness down even more because the grid's power was lower. The world had to put the dimmer switch on to adapt to them, by compassion, otherwise, those lower vibration beings could not be here. This is the definition of hijacking the incarnation grid.

There is no other way to describe this except metaphorically, but it's very real. The council of twelve tried to use CERN — the large Hadron collider in France — to *fudge* the numbers. This is the true spiritual history of the earth. The prime creator audits the true economy here, which is the energetic exchanges and creations against the backdrop of the ruleset in the divine hologram — a *for real* audit — and the ass jacks on the council thought they could fool the prime creator. We have to admire the temerity, and we have to note the prime creator's commitment to his ruleset. Free will is just that. Not even the prime creator can violate the ruleset once the game is in motion. The ruse was seen through by the prime creator, and they were all ejected from the game. All of those people that were part of the deception, the light, too, because the light was also doing some bad things at the time. There are light beings so immersed in the light they only see darkness. They're deep into polarity — zealots — and there's no neutral side between them. They battle just to battle because they've battled for so long they know nothing else. They started — *I'll win at any cost.* When we say *win at any cost* we're no longer light beings. We need to heal, go back to our source, and look at it from a different perspective. This includes the dark ones, too. The situation got so out of whack some dark ones turned out to be of the light, simply because it was the only way to counter the *light.*

Earth is a unique experiment — a binary world with free will — and the drama that has ensued here has amused even the prime creators, who have made mistakes. Yes, a prime creator for a galaxy is not infallible. Earth has proven that. The fifteen beings have proven that.

In our sixty-six planet solar system, Venus has always been the most philosophical society. The Venusians were affected by what was going on here, as were the other sixty-four planets in our solar system, but only the Venusians documented their concern. The Venusian philosophers got together in a massive psychic group-mind which was broadcast. The Venusians are known to declare seventy-two-hour peace periods. They are generally respected in the solar system. At this truce conference, there were philosophers from the light, dark, and neutral perspectives. They all sat down and debated. They don't argue. They just debate. Everybody's side is put on the table for trillions of people to watch. The Venusians are known for philosophy.

Earth's situation was very unique to the Venusian philosophers. If service-to-self ascension happens, the philosophers have no inkling of what it means. It is that new. The multidimensional beings planned and planned. They wanted to usurp a prime creator who is a spark of the universal creator. The universal creator might want service-to-self ascension out of the creation. The Venusians didn't know, but what a lively debate topic. If it was allowed it had to serve a purpose, and it was this which baffled the great Venusian philosophers.

A method of graduation — in this case moved to a time-space where they could be productive — was created for the fifteen. It's called service-to-self ascension, a cosmic left-hand path if you will. It's a concept created in this universe, a product of the free will experiment here. We created a whole new method of ascension. It has since spread to non-free-will universes. It was always a theory no one could prove correct. We did that, we human beings incarnating in this sound and light hologram. Let that sink in. We created something out of our experiences and trials here that we presented to God. It wasn't part of his original creation. This is an important thing to note. It's not all God giving to us. A creation like this multiverse is an opportunity for God to learn and grow. We co-work and co-create new things with our prime creator. It's a glorious and redeeming thing to know for us humans. We have a purpose beyond our understanding. We matter, every one of us.

When this was established, a way out for the fifteen, most of them came here fully. This means the parts of them elsewhere reunited with the parts of them here. These beings can be in more than one place at the same time. We all can, but they're fully conscious of it. Even with the offer of service to self ascension, not all of them moved on. Some of them dug in and continued their attempt to usurp the prime galactic creator here. They fully invested in the earth. These beings were so large they couldn't fit into a single human body. They incarnated into tens of thousands of bodies simultaneously. There are no other parts of them anywhere else. Others still have parts in other places. The ones that are fully invested here, the best guess from the light forces out there is they won't be able to succeed. Earth consciousness will absorb them because they're contracted to be here in some way, but, they've created side contracts that divert earth's main contracts. They're in charge of the incarnation grid. They've tried killing earth sentience and replacing it many times. They can't. Everything fails at some point. Service-to-self ascension for these beings could mean all of their pieces and parts individually ascend and become higher entities. If there's a part away from the planet, the guess is it ascends too. The possibility exists these new parts might become thousands of master avatars that can create more pieces to go to more galaxies.

In the end, there was a kind of compromise reached with the fifteen beings. Three of them were cast to universal nothingness, which is a kind of non-existence. One was asked to share the responsibility of the galaxy by the prime creator, and when the being did this it realized it was not ready and stepped down. Several of them were sent to other young galaxies as prime creators, so they could grow into the role of prime creator. Two remain. They are incarnated within about twenty-five thousand people each. What they will do is unknown. No more can be said about them here. It's best to let them be and finish their cycle here as well as they can.

Rewrites

The earth has had its hard drive wiped and rewritten numerous times. This is a flagrant violation of universal law, but it happens nonetheless. This should tell you everything you need to know about the law. It can be contradicted at a fundamental level, all of it, gravity, aging, time. Nothing is guarding it. It's more of a suggestion than a law. Once broken we own the effect. You break it you buy it. Sometimes people break laws just to see what will happen. It's a learning experience. Did you ever eat dirt as a kid? There's a part of sentience that is forever eating dirt like a child, except the dirt becomes time, cloning, uncreational events, and everything else we can break. One person's evil is another person's experiment. It all depends on our level of awareness. Most people think an alien race taking over the earth is evil. It's an evil imagining — despite the fact it's the undeclared truth of the earth — but we have no problem with mass murder, genocide, and colonization among ourselves. Our worst fears are nothing more than having done to us what we have done to others. Even our imaginations are driven by karma.

The time wars began four hundred and eight thousand years ago, but once time war is introduced time itself becomes meaningless. What happens once time warfare is introduced? All time is changed. Even though the time wars only began four hundred and eight thousand years ago, they now infect the entire fifty million year history of the earth, because the inception of time warfare is the inception of no accurate time, going back to the beginning of Akashic Recording.

This is what is meant by a rewrite. The whole history gets rewritten, not just the history from the commencement of time warfare. Makes sense when we think about it. We are just rarely taxed with thinking about it. The collective unconscious, the *spiritus mundi*, as it was called in Latin, is aware of the time distortions. They are expressed in our popular culture, cinema, science fiction books, and, of course, aspects of this truth are retained by the conscious beings sharing the earth with humanity, unbeknownst to the vast majority of humans on the planet.

The fifteen multidimensional beings who incarnated here became forty percent of our breeding population. Fifteen beings equaled forty percent of humanity. That many human forms were required to fully incarnate one soul. That's how large the multidimensional beings became. At that point, there were almost seventy billion people on earth. This is how the fifteen got soul family status with everyone. They brought in dimensional technology meant only for vessels, installed it on earth, and began experimenting — taking one continent out of a timeline, putting it back into a distant timeline, one by one — to redefine the *first species* of earth.

The first species is a spiritual title recognized by the prime creator, and enforceable in any court of spiritual equity. It has weight and meaning. It means that they who hold the title hold the deed. The first sentient species on a planet is a big deal. There are now seventy-two first species of earth. Every time earth was recaptured in these battles the *light force* tried to rewrite the timelines. There was a problem, though. Once sentience is born it can't be erased. Earth has to adopt it as a first species. The time wars are all about creating the *first sentience*, and the light forces broke the law as much as the dark forces.

Earth is now a warehouse of species and timelines. Atop the seventy-two first species, we have six thousand different refugee species who've come to live in our world because their worlds are being decimated or destroyed. Earth has always been a soul migration spot. Earth is a migration spot because of its impressive graduation timeline. We have one hundred percent free will here. It's very important. There are other worlds where they remember all their past lives. They speak by the time they're four months old. We go through this growing process on earth. It's cherished in other worlds.

The blank Akashic Record is a unique ability of this planet, our precious earth. It's an aspect of the rewrite process, the shadow side of it to be more specific. It started in Lemuria, which was very high consciousness. Earth was its true seventh-dimensional status at that time. It created DNA and invited other species to come to live with her for a while. After some time, they could live above these womb chakras and create DNA, then take it to a new world. This was all done within the unity of the earth's original purpose. All DNA was moved by the law of free will and consent.

Each time free will and consent are violated a contract is signed — you break it you buy it — whether we realize it or not. It's true for us, and it's true for other species as well. It's the only way to learn.

Earth is also capable of physical teleportation. She can move the DNA wisdom created in her womb chakras to a blank Akashic Record planet on the cusp of inviting its first group of souls for coexistence. During the Lemurian times, there were air cities — quite literally cities that floated in the air — ground cities, and as many as five thousand species that came here to work with the earth, create DNA, and propagate that DNA. Earth is a nursery of sorts.

One of the things that has arisen in the consciousness of man is what has been termed the Mandela effect. It's named after the South African freedom fighter and eventual leader of the African National Congress (ANC). The Mandela effect was born as a phrase when a psychic named Fiona Broome said she had memories of South African President Nelson Mandela passing away in prison in the nineteen-eighties. In our actual recorded history, he died in 2013. This would not have been very eventful had not many more people stepped forward to add their consensus, and this is how the *Mandela effect* got coined. It's become so prolific in the cultural vernacular that the foot soldiers of the global narrative have been dispatched, in this instance academe, which has been one of the main enforcers of the global narrative – collective false memories, confabulation, false memory syndrome. It's the job of anyone employed by the global narrative to demystify things because the last thing the controllers want is an outbreak of multidimensional humans.

The Mandela Effect is the karma of all those who have been manipulated throughout time, as well as bleed-through from other times. The system has shifted our reality and moved soul shards onto other realities so our memories would be fragmented. It is a way for the universe to put everything back to neutral and help us find the forgotten pieces of ourselves, the pieces and parts that have been manipulated and put outside of time. We have to get all the fractured pieces — lost and found implicate orders — together for the celestial medium of peace journey. There are versions of ourselves lost in void space who never got resolution. We can resolve that paradox by creating experiences and legacies.

The DNA farming that has gone on here on earth has left time scars. The DNA farmers — Elohims, Reptilians, Orions, Annunaki, Arcturians, Sirians, to name some — had different ways of perceiving the galactic commerce network through technology. They manipulated the flow of energy between star systems with technology, even though they had not achieved celestial medium status in their spiritual journeys. They were entangled observers using technology that simulated unentangled observer technology. This allowed them manipulation within thousands of years instead of millions of years. Those original DNA manipulating beings thought they were gods. They kept manipulating DNA and the flow of energy between celestial sources allowing them to farm all DNA on a grand scale.

The forgotten selves are part of our forgotten workforce. They are trying to get back into the zone where our precognitive workforce can perceive them. They are aspects no longer connected to the nonlinear soul. Their original linear time was erased. They are trying to get out of this erased time back into non-linear time. There is a network of forgotten selves that works together to be remembered. The Mandela effect is a broadcast to all forgotten selves in awareness, unawareness, time, and no-time. Wherever life has gone, even if it has been erased, there is an opportunity, a portal back to the hub of interconnectivity. It can be perceived as the trans-galactic exchange system between eras of light. Those forgotten selves will integrate with our precognitive and post cognitive workforce and no longer be forgotten but remembered and added to our Akashic Record.

These forgotten selves can represent themselves in an infinite number of ways. It all depends on how long they have been forgotten and what gifts they have to offer. Our other selves are the ones searching for the lost Mandela effects. It is our responsibility to indicate to our precognitive and post cognitive workforce that it should be a priority to find every aspect of our forgotten selves up to nine hundred degrees of separation from us in this phase of awakening.

This is the toll the time wars have had upon us. It's never been explained or expressed in our total consciousness expression, which is what we would call fiction and non-fiction. Many times things are allowed into expression through fiction. Sometimes it's because the build-up in the collective human unconscious demands it, so what is done by the global narrative editors is a release of energy, a meaningless catharsis. This is a form of energy harvesting to maintain the global narrative. If they didn't release the energy, like letting steam out of a pipe, it would explode.

Many aspects of consciousness are the result of time warfare and its consequences. When a human being loses a limb they can have sensations related to the missing limb for the rest of their lives. They can even feel the need to scratch the missing limb. Lost timelines and erased histories are like this. They never really go away. We can have a sensation that we have done something, know something, or remember something, but we can not prove it. Many times this can be timeline reclamation. Time is happening all at once. Our past and future lives are being lived right now.

All of these things, no matter how improbable they sound right now, will be openly understood and discussed shortly. It can not be put off anymore. The event has cleared the way for multidimensional consciousness.

Yellow Box

Not many people know about the yellow box. The yellow box is technology to predict humanity's DNA expression over millennia of evolution. It is founder technology. It allowed them to go into the *potential of history* and create small changes to allow co-creative evolution instead of forced evolution. The yellow box predicts the future. It shows the lines of the potential future. There are three yellow boxes in total. Two are controlled by the USA. One is in Las Vegas, one in Pine Gap, Australia. The last is in Germany. All three boxes give a line of potentials. All three must agree. The one in Germany no longer agrees with the other two. Two out of the potential three timelines have a much greater potential, but the yellow box in Germany is discordant with its other two. In seventy years of using the boxes, this has never happened.

As of 2015, they have not agreed. There are too many time travel scenarios, alternate timelines, temporal pollution. The people writing and editing the global narrative — the cabal, the hollow earth races, external sources keeping this homeostasis we're stuck in — have employed time travel manipulation too much. The boxes no longer work together. It's only a matter of time before one of the American-controlled yellow boxes shows an alternate timeline, and all three show unique timelines.

There is a fifth column in the battle to free the earth. They have done some positive time travel, creating a powerful and unpredictable *butterfly effect*. When the two American boxes that are agreeing now no longer agree, the box in Germany will not confirm the controllers' prediction model. When that happens, a very unique scenario occurs: the hollow earth races must exert control over the entire apparatus and infrastructure of control on the surface. Then the externals, positive and negative aliens, have to exert control to keep the hollow earth people underground and the mass apparatus of infrastructure and control here is going to ask: *Whose side do we choose?*

The boxes work on the law of the universe — harmony, frequency, vibration, and the law of attraction and repulsion. If a timeline's potential is positive, its outcome is known, and humanity will naturally be attracted to it. If the boxes show seventy-five potential timelines, seventy-five percent of the people go with it. The other twenty-five percent go the opposite way because they aren't a match. They manipulate timelines and create micro-changes before, during, and after elections, no matter who is president in the United States. The frontman who runs the senate, the Vice President, is energetic as much as a physical seat of power. The Vice President is a ritualistic person who has energy constantly thrown at them, just like the President. The Vice President has a mechanical function in the unseen actions of the cabal.

History has been one-hundred percent rewritten. As multi-functional and multidimensional beings of awareness, we experience parallel timelines as linear. Our linear history is stitched together with pieces taken from all the different timelines. It's managed by the global narrative. The history books are rewritten every thirty to forty years.

Many times when they put us on a different timeline a lot of women have been pregnant fifty times with an off-world fetus, or a clone of themselves. They may not realize it. Egg and sperm can come together in an external source. The zygote is put inside the women for six to seven hours then taken out. Sometimes this is done two-hundred to three-hundred times to couples. It's done so the fetus has a signature frequency matching this linear time. This allows switching to other times. They use sperm and egg technology as part of the source-time frequency in breeding programs.

We are a farm. They farm us for our easily weaponized consciousness. Indoctrinated belief systems are used to put us onto alternate timelines. They never tell us we've been transferred. The indoctrinated believe what they're told. Timeline jumping is so remote in public discourse most people don't even have a framework to question such a thing. We have all these genetic programs from the off-world, good, bad, and indifferent, as well as the genetic hollow earth programs which keep us trapped on the farm.

Earth has many things like the yellow boxes. It's a galactic scavenger hunt for many of the off-world races. They come here looking for technology from the many wars and life forms that have lived here. It's scattered all over the planet, going right back to Lemuria. Since the misalignment between the boxes, we have an unpredictable future. This is an opportunity for the earth. It is an effect of the event, and it is the beginning of the prime creator's audit effect.

As dark as the world may look, we are on the cusp of indescribable change. Most of the control apparatus is gone or losing efficacy. It may seem like the opposite is happening, but that's only because the remaining control apparatus has to become more overt. The subtler forms of control, the fourth-dimensional control, the fifth-dimensional control, have waned. They're not showing it, but they're terrified. Many of the negatives left after the event, after the quarantine grid on earth was lifted. Those remaining are the zealots, the fanatics. They will have to have power taken from them.

Light and Dark

There has been so much turmoil here it's nearly impossible to distinguish between light and dark. There are light beings in fake dark beings and dark beings in fake light beings, and then we have fake light beings who are both. It's been nearly impossible to escape the quagmire that is earth, the false god system, the sub-tracked incarnation process, and the outright hijacking of everything natural and true. What you think are spiritual masters are not, even if they might believe they are spiritual masters. The deception runs deep. This is the result of the free will experiment here, centered on the jewel of this universe – earth.

Most of the religious leaders of the world are vile, misguided, or fully complicit actors in the great deception and repression. This may be difficult to hear, but truth like medicine is often bitter. The root of the deception has been the root of consciousness, our search for meaning and purpose. Religions are the mental corollary to genetic manipulations, just another way to keep us dumbed down.

An interesting case of a deep fake in the light and dark dance is John of God, the Brazilian healer. He had a very colorful public life. Hollywood stars like Oprah Winfrey endorsed him. He even had a difficult relationship with the Vatican, a very powerful social and political force in Brazil. They were instrumental in getting him arrested. He spent time in prison. In the end, he was arrested for child trafficking and other heinous crimes. He was running a baby farm and a eugenics program. He wanted to populate the world with his seed. Only about ten percent of his story came out in the news. The rest is too unsavory and shall remain absent from these pages as well. Whether John came in with a negative agenda or the Vatican broke him into using his ability to their service is irrelevant. He is a perfect example of a dark force masquerading as a light force.

If a true light force incarnates and leaves a legacy like a book, the moment he or she dies a cult forms and the same disinformation enthusiasts co-opt the movement and teachings. If it's happened once, it's happened a hundred times on this planet. There were other people here as *fake* masters. This is easy for an accomplished magician, wizard, or an initiate of a mystery school on assignment. Consciousness is so low if someone even has a little astral ability they can pass themselves off as a *man of god.* The Ayurveda and Taoist systems are good but incomplete. There has been no way out of here for a long time. Anyone who claims otherwise is lost in one or another of the many inner deceptions. Contemplate this for a moment. We have been taught in most of the world's systems that life is nothing but suffering and these systems can lead us to a better and permanent place. So the gift of life bequeathed to us by the prime creator is worthless, to be lived with contempt, and only used as an opportunity to escape life by incarnation. It's uniform in both the east and west. Most of our instruction comes from our fetus in the womb plan, which is always about karma resolution, but the karmic system only operates correctly in a reality that has not been hijacked.

No actual masters are walking our planet. It's a rule. Many of them broke the rules in the past and were ejected from the game. The prime creator doesn't play any games or have any favorites. There is no nepotism with the prime creator because we're all equally related to the prime creator. It's also worth noting that no human can attain god consciousness. A human being can encompass an aspect of the creator, but no more. A lot of seekers see the nonsense in their birth culture, like the North Americans who run to an Indian ashram, but they put blinders on, stop using their critical thinking, and never see the bullshit on the ashram. It's just that bad. It would be great to have a better report, but the opportunity for spiritual growth has been this bleak for quite some time.

Many of the native cultures were quite advanced, and that's why they were murdered. That can be accepted as a general rule — those with real knowledge were killed. This was an ancillary benefit of the European expansion, the annihilation of native cultures. They were autonomous. The plan of the global narrative was interdependence. Autonomy had to be destroyed.

Others have figured out the subtleties. They help us plan our contracts so we can get in here and be powerful. There are ascended masters who help us plan our lives a thousand lifetimes ahead of time, ten thousand lifetimes ahead. Many people are part of the resistance of free earth. Each person who has been planning hundreds of lifetimes is the resistance of free earth. Their purpose is to find the soul codes among all of our commonality of species and then complete them. Once we have a complete soul code as a species, domination and control lose their most important tool, which is the ability to keep us separate as soul families. But all of this is coming to an end now. The dance between light and dark is almost over.

We reached our peak of divisiveness early in the twenty-first century. A quarantine grid is enforced now. There are vessels in our atmosphere taking our consciousness and reinvesting it into the earth, slowly raising the energies of earth, like trickle-charging a battery. If they raised it too fast, some people on this planet couldn't exist here, and they would fade out. Our galactic assistants don't want that to happen. They want the graduating classes. It's all about enough consciousness here to accept the first two stages of the dreamtime events we have, which lead to the harder parts of consciousness to accept. Very soon the dreamtime awakening will happen. People will begin to have dreamtime together, and they will be conscious of it. This will wobble the narrative dominance of the pseudo-scientific paradigm we live in now. It will strike directly at the subject-object supremacy of thought and rhetoric in the public space. People will have unity experiences that begin to dissolve the false barriers.

They can't sell us into slavery anymore. That's what the quarantine is about. The quarantine has many levels. We have diseases here that aren't created by man. These diseases were purposely brought here. If a human being is taken off-world now, they could spread a pan-galactic virus that could kill trillions. It has happened in the past. Trillions were killed.

The original function of CERN was to *fudge the numbers* of the prime creator's audit, but it had other functions, as well. It was a teleportation device. The negatives would try to teleport earth back to the densest part of its galactic journey. The people in that dense part would dream the rest of the solar system back to them. We are co-creating on the graduation timeline. All the other planets in the solar system are intricately linked to our graduating timeline. Co-creating spirits in that timeline can bring us all back.

Both sides, light and dark, broke the most fundamental rules here. The whole human race was taken on a roller coaster ride by zealots on the light and the dark sides. Rules are broken all the time here. You might even say the free will dream space was created to break rules, rules of harmony, rules of love, rules of equity, and those rules were broken so we could learn the balance, the lesson, but there are mistakes, and then there are *mistakes*. The level of chaos on earth has been epic, and with no clear spiritual value. Beings on the light and dark side have been ejected from this galactic ascension machine called earth, and they don't get to be a part of the graduating timeline, and this is both the light and dark beings. Both sides were doing nefarious things to alter the prime creator's will. They'd been experiencing the polarity of light and dark without the respite of neutrality for so long they lost their way.

At this point, the prime creator used what's known as the *walk-in rule*. Those who got ejected were replaced by new souls who took over all contracts and timeline functions. That was the first replacement of the management system. The second layer of replacement comes when the beings who are part of this contractual system of domination and control are going to be replaced with neutral beings with no political objectives, dogmas, or spiritual concepts. They simply see the information and the resolve is putting us as a species in a complete soul code. The galactic ascension machine has always been about taking the two-thousand three-hundred species warring over this planet and making them into a single species. When that happens we go back out to our races and bring the DNA wisdom they've been trying to hoard for themselves.

It might be hard to see right now, but it will become more and more manifest. The exposed darkness of the world is revolting to many now, child trafficking, transhumanism, mass murder, the alien disclosure, the litany of disclosures that started a couple of decades ago. It's the slow unfolding of the truth, bitter medicine indeed, but it has to be recognized. It has to be seen. Only then will people understand how badly we have been deceived.

The artificial intelligence movement on earth now is a replay of what took Atlantis and Lemuria down. There's a lot of repetition in the recent timeline. It's an aspect of futility, which everyone who has been trapped in this false god system is feeling. The dramas being played out now are like a song on the Akashic jukebox we have to play again because there's unresolved karma. Technology passed from one generation to the next created the failures of our societies on earth. Society isn't balanced between light, dark, and neutral. There's an overwhelming number of low vibration people in domination and control who use the technology to pursue personal power and ambition.

This will not last much longer, but the horror, the degradation of the human, the vain pursuit of the superman in defiance of our supernatural abilities will persist for a while longer. It will reach a point where people will become numb to it, but in becoming numb they will shut down their divine heart connection to life, and then, in the darkest hour, it will break like a fever, and a mad rush to spiritual equilibrium will happen. There's no other way. The negatives in charge of the world now have been abandoned by their multidimensional support and left to themselves they will reveal themselves as the frauds and counterfeits they are. It's a sour victory, and there will be no vengeance by human hands. They will simply be removed in disgust and the portion of the human race slated for graduation will move on as well. The earth will go back to its original function and purpose. Enough has been enough.

Orion and Sirian Wars

The Orion and Sirian war was the last galactic war earth was involved with. It sounds strange to talk about a war that is not officially in our record, though it is being discussed quite a bit in disclosure and exopolitics circles, it happened, and it lasted a little more than half a million years, persisting in some ways right until today.

In 2006 we could have been done with this war. The Sirian, Gray, and Orion wars depleted the forces significantly. The light forces did not have the physical strength to come here and kick the negatives out, tear the power out of their cold dead hands, if you will, and, at the same time, they discovered a massive layer of corruption within their light societies.

They were using DNA smuggling from the earth trade to save other races. There are many races out there on the verge of death, infertile, incapable of breeding, the result of using cloning technology for eighty thousand years. They don't have sex organs or know how to have children. They do everything by test tube and expect the soul family to come in. So many of their soul family are stuck here. They're not inviting them, because their soul family rules are so specific.

These societies are desperate, down to a few thousand of their species remaining, so they used this underground smuggling network — the fifteen multidimensional beings — to kidnap humans off this world and harvest their DNA and the soul codes from them. All to save their species. They called it graduating.

There we see one of the great galactic moral paradoxes. Is what they did wrong, in the context of saving an entire species? Yes. It's wrong.

Is it understandable? Yes, it is understandable when you reach the desperation of the last of the species. Yet, at the same time, they decided to go into cloning; they didn't listen to the better counsel in their species; they didn't slow down when they saw warning signs over generations; they didn't think of a backout plan from cloning; they made a free-will decision; they created the karma. Tough love? It's the love of the prime creator. All the direction is inside us — all sentient species — and it's our job as a race to stay on the spirit road to higher consciousness in harmony with universal law. They kidnapped humans.

When it was discovered how deep the corruption went, that light beings were in the human smuggling business, it was the beginning of the understanding of how insidious and how deep it went. Insidious. The Orion species are soul family to us. They were refugees here. We were refugees on their planet. They were both the good guys and the bad guys, and so were we. The wars are about soul societies and races pitted against one another, a galactic coliseum, each race throwing the other to the lions and cheering. It was eerie, the darkness within darkness, a galactic hanging garden — the indecency of it, the totality of it, all to yield to the reality of it — that which exists now exists forever. As much as we would like to gift ourselves the power of destruction, it is not being offered, but we may hurt ourselves in perpetuity. That is allowed.

Rebirth is the adjudication of many things, but in the end, it is the greatest mercy. Until the light comes on inside us, it's all maintenance down here. We will be perpetually maintaining what we destroy — build it break it. It's a guaranteed economy, and as much as they say it's a free market, they don't take any chances.

The Orion wars came to a head in 2006. The war was technology versus spirit. The spiritual side adopted some technology. The technology side refused all spirit. They were creating beings with no trees-of-life – clone wars. It was an abomination, a violation so deep it was an affront to universal law.

They began kidnapping people from other worlds to become the perfect ship engines. People were taken for psychic energies they possess, taken from the corpus then implanted in a ship to be the drive energy. We produce extraordinary things on this planet. We are extraordinary beings. We're the last to believe it ourselves. The technologists violated sovereign free will. We were just a part with a number to them, an apathy so diabolical as to be anathema to spirit. When the wars came to a head some three-hundred and fifty planets counted themselves among it.

In one stunning move, the technologists released all their captured beings, their slave force throughout several thousand worlds. They just let them go like Castro emptied his jails and asylums when America was taking Cuban refugees. It was the tactical genius of a collective unbound by even codes of honor in combat, as only those completely devoid of empathy can be. A massive refugee nightmare ensued — an unspeakable situation. In 2006 reptilian vessels were forcing themselves into the solar system. The forces of light were trying to finish the last of the Orion wars. This was the field of battle.

That is just one cycle of war, a recent one. There have been many. War has degraded everyone, but there always seemed to be one group taking it a step-down, less honor, less dignity, less respect for the prime creator and its laws, while still respecting our free will right to war. It wasn't so much that the wars were untenable within a free will, it was how much we grew into war, how multidimensional we made it, traversing even time itself in skips and jumps as a tactical map of warfare, Caesar's tent if it were the galaxy itself.

This is how deeply war got into us. It was all war all the time. It never stopped. Look around you. Almost any item you see had its origin in military research, including the knife you cut your food with.

Annunaki

Nibiru or Planet X is real. It was a real situation with a real planet. It's been moved dozens of times. Technology was installed on it that keeps it out of phase. This is so our fear does not manifest it again. In the past, the main domination and control beings had pieces and parts of themselves throughout the timeline which could communicate to the central hive location.

Zecharia Sitchin's first three books are very accurate. His timelines are off. Sitchin's work was co-opted. when Sitchin wrote his books he had a multidimensional being helping him translate the texts. He was a highly spiritual person who had a purpose in coming to earth. He is accurate up to *The Wars of Gods and Men*. The timing is a little off because earth has changed time streams so many times.

The Annunaki were lured here some twenty-five million years ago, relative newcomers in context to the galactic history given in this book's history of the earth. Their planet, Nibiru, is a free-roaming galactic entity planet. It has a drive inside it that does not need a solar system to support it. They have a different version of a planetary drive. We have a unity consciousness drive. They have a dimensional drive. The consciousness only needs leadership to function psychically with the crystalline technology of the dimensional drive. They go anywhere they want, and do whatever is within their free will to do.

One of the dark ones, the fifteen multidimensional beings from the beginning, the bane of the Lemurians, lured them from where they were with carrots and sticks. As they were drawn in they saw leftover technology and destroyed worlds. They followed one to the next. Finally, they came to our solar system. Nobody was defending it. All of the light and dark forces had exhausted themselves and could not fight anymore. Earth was abandoned except for what was left of us. This was before the rise of Atlantis. Lemuria had fallen again through multiple timeline wars.

The Annunaki were baffled. There was all this technology scattered about and a bunch of primitive people — us — with high spiritual technology. The technology didn't match us, but the Annunaki couldn't piece together the forensics of earth. That's when they realized they were us and we were them. We were DNA-related. It dawned on them too late that they had been lured here.

The stargates of the sun are the passageway into our solar system, but an approaching race has to have spiritual relations, DNA relations to get into a solar system. The Annunaki were a free-roaming galactic planet that came into our solar system. They never knew they had DNA relations with us. The beings who lured them knew. It trapped them in the incarnation grid, stripped them of their most powerful psychics, and forced them into a reincarnation cycle. The next most powerful layer became the new DNA inputs for the skinsuit technology we had here. The Annunaki DNA and the soul codes were wanted. The Annunaki had traveled all over the universe with their planet. They were a rich harvest of soul codes.

The main control beings have been trying to collect soul codes. Soul codes determine our DNA and soul relations to a solar system. They determine where we can go. If we have only lived on ten planets, we can only go to those ten planets on a soul level. If we want to go to more, we have to incarnate into all of them. The dark ones were drawing people here who had soul codes from all over. The Annunaki had soul codes that opened up the universe.

Sitchin was correct about mining earth, but it was not about the materials. It was that the energy in the materials needed to go somewhere else. Earth-based souls who had migrated away would sense the energy of the gold somewhere else and be lured back into the machine. That's the control system here. The Annunaki still have free will. They did not understand the scale of the game they were brought into.

The Annunaki already had enough skinsuit technology that they were a little bit of everything. Not everything, but they had enough. They looked similar to humans, but several breeds of them chose different DNA patterns even though they were the same species. They could do anything they wanted to their DNA. The false light teachings essentially began by bringing the Annunaki here. False light beings and false light technology were created by the Annunaki and then spread to the rest of the planets of domination and control through the womb chakras of the earth.

Almost every religion and spiritual teaching on the planet has been affected by the false light technology and the false gods created by the Annunaki. It's a reincarnation system wherein the departed go through the false light and reincarnates. It is an absolute perversion and abuse of creational law. The lack of teaching on this planet and the imbalances created by violation of creational law have created a unique being, the human being, but our consciousness has been so redacted it's almost a negative net gain. Religion became the control system until the contemporary global narrative began to overtake it with the European enlightenment, Industrial Revolution, and our present man-machine option through our genetic tampering, nanotechnology, and transhumanism, all of which is the end run of a spiritually bankrupt people and social system.

Part III

End Game

Chapter 5

Twenty-first Century

Here Be Dragons

Dragons are real. Not only are they real, but they are also an integral part of the creation. They exist in our collective consciousness but only as fiction, fable, myth. Like everything else we have relegated to mythology, they once co-existed with us on this planet. Conceptualize dragons this way — a very intense piece of fabric, every little piece, patch, and stitch means something, and all of those pieces, patches, and stitches are the fabric of dragons. They are part of the placenta of energy the earth gives off so we can work in her reality, not just here on this planet, but every other planet. All planets, galaxies, and universes use some form of residual dragon image for their universal expression of exchange.

Every planet creates beings of photonic light. One of these beings of photonic light holds the energy of the god or goddess of that planet and its belief system. These beings are dragons, architects of all that is that we know as creation. Their function is to create reality templates, dream space, and program a reality. They were highly involved with DNA commerce, spiritual vehicles for soul commerce.

The original dragons earth spawned who held the original templates of this planet were kicked off the earth. Then there were the timeline genocides. We now have over ten thousand species of dragons from different planets. They hold DNA lineages from all these planets as well as some of the original earth DNA lineage after the timeline genocide. Some of the original dragons that held the lineage of the DNA of earth templates also came back. Fifteen to eighteen percent of humans on this planet have access to this energy.

The dragons were lured onto this planet through a technology that imprinted on the actual DNA skinsuit of a human through a tattoo, sacred geometry formations that attracted dragon energy into the human form, and by the time they realized they were in the human form, it was too late. Millions were lured then caught in the reincarnation cycles. The tattoo was a DNA photonic light technology that was imprinted onto the DNA skinsuit. Thirty to thirty-five percent of the human beings in those skinsuits remember. They formed triad dragon armies. They have memories from the beginning of the earth's journey, and they returned now, in the end, to make sure the original plan of this earth comes to fruition.

Dragons are our elemental link to this planet. Every planet creates them. This planet trapped them inside the archon grid. The dragon triad armies were born in about three hundred B.C. in secret. They jumped back in time as many as thirty-one million years and forward to 2009 for the last updates to dragon families in human bodies that had not resolved karma. The dragon triad's purpose was to reach out to other planets, dimensions, and universes to find beings who had created karma here then left our universe with unresolved karma. For us to reach a point where the event could happen this had to occur. They reached out to thousands and eventually millions of worlds and other galaxies and universes so that all karma created within the sixty-six prime planets of timeline drama could resolve karma.

We live in a world of predation. It's part of the spiritual contract here. Vegetarianism and its zealots are practicing spiritual style, not spiritual substance. If you feel the need to stop eating meat or lower your meat intake, that's fine, too, but ignore these eastern zealots who say you can't advance beyond a certain point spiritually if you eat meat. Native cultures ritualized the hunt and treated the animal as sacred. Modern corporate agriculture and meat processing is quite bad karma, but it's being done intentionally by the negatives on the planet to keep the frequency lower.

If a cat eats a mouse the cat is blissful. It does not have a conscience about killing the mouse. It has a different level of unawareness of karma. When dragons and humans in dragon frequency take on predation to balance karma they are similarly exempt from effect because it's about the remedy and resolution. It's their spiritual duty to the planet, the solar system, the galaxy, and even into other universes.

The dragons that got trapped here found ways to constitute the dragon soul in human soul families. The most notable dragon clan in our recorded history, however inaccurate that history, is Genghis Khan. He materialized on the earth. He was not born. His Mongol hordes operated multidimensionally and jumped around in time, going as far back as thirty million years, and right up until 2009, all as part of the karmic reconciliation that would bring about the event.

Earth had been reached out to and attacked thousands of times. They tried to kill her and take her out of her own body, and there has to be a response to that karma, even from the earth, and her choice was to spawn artificial gangs such as Genghis Khan, Alexander the Great, and many others so she could begin conquering her timelines back, through her beings, and then impress what would survive through history.

The dragon lineages brought the chi teachings fully into the martial arts, the power of the breath to make the body diamond-hard or as subtle as water. The chi is the dragon energy manifest on the earth, and the triads centered themselves on these teachings.

Little Dragon

Bruce Lee's name was Lee Xiao Long. In Chinese culture, the family name is said first. Xiao is pronounced *shao*. It means little. Long is pronounced *longe*. It means dragon. His name was Lee Little Dragon.

There was a psychic pheromone to Bruce Lee. When we have soul family relations and connections with people at such an intense level, these psychic pheromones can take over to resolve karma. These psychic pheromones were used to take over different skinsuit organizations. They could go to the top of a hierarchical order. They could start a mass assembly of souls to take on a project — war, building a temple, irrigating land, or teaching people about the breath of life.

Bruce Lee trained like no one else in the world. He created machines for his body so he could do maneuvers with his feet or his arms. There were types of speed bags he used, a special shield he carried so he could kick things people were holding.

The technology to capture him moving didn't come around until the late eighties, cameras that could go down to the number of frames per second that could see, moment to moment, the motion of what he was doing. He was a real action star. People knew by the way he could construct a fight scene, like the big fight scenes in so many of his movies where the whole dojo comes after him, or everyone in the ice house comes after him, choreographed martial arts in full frequency flow of the psychic mind.

When the Mongolian hoards set themselves upon the conquest of China, there was a uniting of the dragon empire and the dragon emperors, which was where much of the martial arts training began, at the local community level. Certain types of people were needed in new dragon clans, separate from the old trapping dragon clans. Bruce Lee was an example of the next generation that survived.

In the film, *Dragon*, we are told Bruce Lee was dressed as a girl when he was a baby and an infant. The reason for this given in the film is that the family believed it was cursed by a demon, and, based on young Bruce's inner life, the parents might well have assumed he was being demonically harassed. The truth is that Bruce was such a powerful soul that time and incarnation agents were aware of him. We may think of these beings as remote viewers operating on the astral.

It's important to take a moment and realize this point. The incarnation grid is policed. The dragon lineages were dormant in the west. Nobody in control wanted an Asian dragon to spread the dragon soul codes in the west. Every time we as human beings get a soul code awakening, we grow in awareness. Bruce Lee, along with Genghis Khan, were instrumental in bringing in the dragon energy leading up to this very special moment we now live within, a moment made possible by countless sacrifices and heroic efforts, not all of which were recorded, and certainly, many of them remain unknown, aside from the Akashic Record, but all can be celebrated in Bruce Lee, at least the heroes of the dragon clans.

Bruce was born into a dragon lineage. His mother and father and lineage going back thousands of years had dragons in it. When his soul as a dragon came into the incarnation grid and was forced into a human DNA skinsuit, he chose a skinsuit, as the dragon soul he was, that had other dragon representations in it, so there was some type of memories that could still keep him connected to his original dragon concept. Bruce Lee is a natural dragon of earth.

The dragons of earth were kicked out. Many of them were killed. Others of those dragons kicked out bred with other dragons, and then those dragons returned to earth and bred with other natural dragons, which made the second-born dragon. Bruce Lee was about the eightieth-born dragon from the beginning of dragon removal from earth. There are some eighty generations of dragon lineages blended into a human DNA skinsuit.

This human skinsuit was highly tuned to be able to take a dragon's soul, and if that dragon's soul chiseled the body the way Bruce Lee did, more and more density of the soul would come in to create the mythical being that he is by essence. Dragons are elemental systems of control for the reality in which we function. When you have a soul inside a skinsuit that's directly linked to the planet and is in an awakening dragon process, it realizes through its sovereignty it can influence the whole world.

He went through the forgetting like everyone else born, went through different stages of remembering. A dragon remembers differently than regular children. His sentience was activated at three years old, so he would have the earliest desire to begin knowing the body.

His movies were the highest form of spiritual alchemy possible without doing magic itself. He was telling the story of the dragon, the story of the martial artist. His daily tool became the camera and the stuntmen. The strategy behind it changed the world. Those fight scenes were laced with his psychic pheromone. When you are that powerful of a personality, you have that much pull in the world, you have a very unique opportunity to help people change by sticking to the message of learning what's inside your body, a spirit of great power, and that spirit of great power changes this reality. It affects people. They ask themselves, *can I change?*.

Coming into that realized power is important now. Martial arts, artwork, drawing, painting, boat riding, bicycle riding, creative writing, all things which can be practiced with the same mindset as Bruce Lee – training the body to bring more and more of our spirit in so we can be realized in the self at all levels.

Bruce Lee came in with a massive soul family that had a dragon's soul and dragon's lineage in it. Jimi Hendrix was the dragon energy as well, born into a DNA skinsuit that had not had dragon lineage in it before. This is why Jimi Hendrix burned out the way he did. His physical skinsuit couldn't handle the amount of creativity he had. The musical genius and the skill shift with the guitar are as mystical and magical as Bruce Lee in fight scenes.

Bruce Lee was murdered for a very specific reason. The next movie he was going to do was going to trigger a mass awakening. He needed to be removed from the potential of that timeline. The controllers of our world went to him and tried to buy him out. He was not for sale. So the controllers of our world went to the triads. The triads then went to Bruce Lee and said, *do as you're told or we will come after you.* His response was simple and direct — *send your masters.* It was as if even before the fight commenced he set the terms for minimal casualties. Send your best, he told them, knowing if he beat them then they would understand he was immovable, and better to kill some of the best than many of the underlings. Even in the direst of circumstances, he allowed the best possible outcome for his enemies in his planning. Dragons are spiritual. They fight. They kill. Yet they want the best outcome for all parties. We must conflict, yes, but we can arrive at a conclusion by the natural law remedy of combat with minimal loss of life. It is everything a hero is or can be.

They did just that. They sent their masters — sword masters, hand combat masters, master gunfighters. He killed them all. This has never been said, the truth of Bruce Lee's life. In most instances, the warrior lore in society is greatly exaggerated. In the case of Bruce Lee, his true lore exceeds the half-century-long fascination with his life and the many rumors that have been told. He was a dragon in flesh.

After a number of the triad masters were killed, the triads retreated from global alliance and control for a generation of reflection – thirty years — to rebuild the lineages and generational wisdom and power Bruce Lee destroyed. They didn't think they could lose their masters.

Bruce Lee took out the highest masters contracted to kill him, so the controllers of our world had to ensure he didn't survive. They put a chemical in his water. It opened him up to a black magic attack. They set three or four thousand hardcore Satanic practitioners upon him. It was a globally coordinated attack. Bruce Lee killed many of the attackers. He was able to kill them on the astral, the most advanced practitioners of ritual black magic, which involved human and child sacrifice, basically the entirety of the Illuminati Cabal. His power was that great, but the little dragon did fall in the end. His story and his fight for humanity don't stop there, though.

When Bruce Lee was murdered, when he was removed from the time stream, he was on a path of destiny. His *I am* presence being removed from here allowed his dragon soul to transcend the incarnation and reincarnation grid. He tore a hole in the archon incarnation grid controlling the planet. It created a path to direct incarnation into dragon DNA lineages. He brought the dragons in to resolve karma. He created a secondary portal entrance for souls to get onto the earth. His soul is holding the space even now.

When a person is removed from the time stream by the controllers, that person is not going to incarnate the next hour, year, or generation. Bruce Lee knew he would be removed before the peak of his time. He left as much of himself as possible — books, philosophy, films. He got so much material out that on the other side he is now doing even more work. He counsels in dreams those who connect with his material while alive.

His son, Brandon, also died young. He inherited the mission of his father, embodying it perfectly in his breakthrough film, *The Crow.* The film was about the corruption of our system and the resurrection of a spiritually vengeful spirit. The central character comes back to life, sent back from the grave with a spiritual mission. It was the perfect definition of his life. It invoked the dragon through sacred vengeance, but again, like his father, within the absolute dignity and honor of the dragon. The karmic balance was done through cinema, storytelling, creativity. Brandon was also a dragon — two generations of an ancient dragon lineage who deeply affected this timeline and prepared us for the moment in which we live.

Moon

The moon, like the earth, is hollow from the fourth dimension up. It's an energetic place in which we can co-create and exist. The moon was a great shield for the earth, protecting it from the energies of three galaxies — the Milky Way, Andromeda, and Sirius. Sirius and Andromeda are the closest to our Milky Way galaxy. The edges of their magnetic fields meet. This is where the solar system is. Earth is a ship in our solar system. They are constantly in attract and repulse mode and never collide, three galaxies in the three-dimensional space. In the fifth dimension, they exist in many places. Earth is a doorway, the gene stock for everywhere.

The moon allows the three galaxies and the planets in this solar system to co-create, to be anchored here, and keeps them all in the same dreamtime and space. The moon is made up of the highest technology and energy beings to keep the three galaxies in karmic exchange for the motion to expand. The moon was the linchpin to hold the three galaxies together. It kept the earth's energy in place. The moon was meant to loop between the parts of the galaxies, to work as a delivery system for plants and animals, and to seed other planets by these higher-dimensional beings. The moon has been destroyed in conflicts. There are two massive crystalline objects inside, schools of ascended masters teaching us the value of dreamtime. One teaches us the co-creative value of the dreamtime. The other teaches us the value of experiencing the third and fourth-dimensional parts of our galaxy. This is where we get our passport to become co-creator among the stars.

Many ascended masters on other planets have missions to spread knowledge and wisdom to other species when they die. They become knowledge crystals when they pass. Dozens of them go into a crystal, creating a hive mind many of us experience in dreamtime. Ascended masters are trying to get us to work together. We talk to the hive mind, all of them at once, like angels. Ascended masters are ephemeral. They can not exist in this world. They wait for us to finish our learning cycle then move on. We are the next ascended masters. Our mission is to maintain peace – no war — for seven generations.

The moon is our immigration office to get off this planet as the great migration of soul begins — the galactic nursery of earth, through the incarnation process, gets us our passports, which we present at the moon, then depart for the planets and galaxies to adapt our consciousness. There's a crystalline city inside the moon, a dreamworld created for the moon. It's out of phase with our reality. The moon was created by a dreamtime society. It manifested out of the dream world from one universe to another so this universe could have an experience of co-creation. Many planets in our galaxy are mobile, but the moon inside their consciousness, their third eye is us because we share incarnation rituals and rules with it. For those of us who want to reawaken that being in the moon, we have to step into the out-of-phase crystal city through remote viewing and projection in a loving space. The gate to our future generations is there through dreams, to our moon, our planet, and our repeating incarnation cycles.

The native Americans called it the moon lodge, where we go in our dreamtime. There is dreamtime here on earth, as well. There's also a moon lodge time women connect through their wombs, which can have children, baby spirits from other galaxies, and universes who go through the moon. They stop there and have their nursery to plan incarnation rituals.

In the procession of the equinox, the moon has what is called a quad wobble; it creates four different sound waves. These four sound waves have eight points in the spherical communication, creating harmony. Depending on the vibration our soul is at, we sing to that chorus differently to access the galactic record of our incarnation rule. It's like an intermediate area where we can understand our soul on a higher level to deal with the final incarnation contracts we created. It's an ambassadorial place between places. Many other species have energetic homes on the moon.

The moon can manifest even ninth-dimensional beings. It's like a hotel, spaceship, cruise liner, galactic ascension machine. Whoever we are in the multiple universes, we may live on the moon. There are several thousand layers of beings existing.

Our solar system has been moved twelve times. The moon we have now is where it was founded in this galaxy. We were brought to this moon. When the solar system was assembled, they looked for the most powerful galactic mind planets one stage away from the ninth dimension, after which planets become stars. They paired a young star with very dominant planetary minds, brought them all here, where the moon is, and made the solar system. There was a battle. Earth was beginning its galactic nursery phase, creating a large plant, amoeba, sand, and water life to seed other planets. The moon was the earth's protector. It had energies that allowed beings from three separate galaxies to come here and make contracts. The moon was a meeting place for soul groups to commence karmic exchange, to co-create and co-exist together.

Hollow Earth

The hollow earth is a series of tunnels on the surface that lead to lower layers into the crust. There's the inner earth, and there are the crustal societies — societies on the edge of living in the graduation timeline but are still within the hollow earth energy system. These are like the ant people of Native American lore. Great insectoid species have been living on earth, nurturing our species, not evil in any way, shape, or form. They are a heart-based species who share dream space through a queen. There are many of these insectoid species who have come from the hollow earth, migrated to the graduation timeline, then bred with us so we could have soul-relations to the queens of heart energy below who are directly linked to earth mother sentience. We shouldn't be afraid of them.

We're all a single species on this earth. We need to complete our soul codes. The system of domination and control makes we don't have a complete soul family in our existence. When we have a complete soul family we are unstoppable. The hollow earth wants us to know that.

We intuitively follow our inner guidance to find our soul families. People will just show up. We will just recognize them. When this happens the human race goes to the next level, or a significant portion thereof. We will be opened to the ancient knowledge right before us all the time. There are stargates based on the womb chakras of the earth. A stargate can open in a womb chakra. DNA wisdom and people can be transported through our sun to any planet or solar system that has our soul codes. This world has a complete set of soul codes for all galaxies.

It's what everyone wants, the soul codes to the galaxies. It's why this drama has been going on and on, why there has been so much chaos, so much time warfare, such an absence of peace. Some galaxies aren't even created yet and we still have the soul codes to them.

The hollow earth and the Agartha network are to make sure there's unity consciousness spreading among people, facilitating dreamtime to communicate with people, to be dreamtime protectors. The Agartha network includes off-world species. Off-world species are our soul family, too. Some are good, some bad, some neutral. We have to come to the understanding that we're the reflection of them, and they are the reflection of us. We're all soul family. The Agarthan network is the ambassadorial spot where these species can gather together in unity consciousness, so we can all see these reflections of ourselves. We can hold galactic councils in a peaceful state and resolve karma. Many of us are gonna be asked to be emissaries or ambassadors. We are going to go forth as the first layer of the graduating students to say — *This is what I've learned. This is my life story.* The hollow earth is to hold the information for seven future generations who come in after the system of domination and control is ended. They're the ones who must oversee the backlog of immigrants who could not incarnate here, all the people stuck in the astral world.

There are four phases of the event. The first phase is shared dreamtime. The second phase is the experience of dÃľjÃă vu on a mass scale, as well as dreams. The third phase is where we begin separating realities. The lower density people will dream themselves into a local reality. The higher-density people will dream themselves into a higher-density reality so that they can begin to be more in touch with their manifesting, co-creating powers. This will be done through dreamtime. You may have a friend that disappears for a week and comes back a whole different person. We won't have complete change until everyone experiences it. All of us have to work together and remove soul contracts with the system of domination and control. This is what the third and fourth phases are — we all claim our sovereign free will.

The hollow earth people will appear on the earth, and we'll instantly recognize them when they're allowed to be on the surface world on the graduating timeline. They're the ones who are going to take over our court system. Our court system is corrupt from the top down. It's meant to cannibalize its people and put them into corporate slavery or physical slavery. These will be called spiritual courts of equity. Our ancestors manifest in a full presence and allow what's been done to us to be read into the fullness of the Akashic Record so we can fully get the healing that's needed by getting our sovereign free will.

All of the conflicts in the Arab world are about preventing seven womb chakras from opening up. They have violence and war on them for an extended period, with the major exchange-for-value systems depositing taxed soul energy into those sacred geometry buildings and ancient technologies that have been there since the Atlantean fortification days. Those womb chakras are the ones that are going to open first. The controllers have always known that. Those are the places that have to have a war on the surface, to prevent the earth's unity consciousness from reaching out through all of the chakras. It's like putting a cork in it.

We have been on a unified timeline since June of 2011, but we — those of us here right now — live all of our past, present, and future lives simultaneously, so when we begin to understand that layer, combined with the time wars layer, we can end all the time wars in the unity consciousness of global dreamtime.

Free Earth Resistance

In the early twentieth century, when the Industrial Revolution hit, the time travel factions began to co-opt the governments on the largest scale. Military budgets had multiple projects underneath them, layered and hidden. Those projects had black projects — deep black projects – and they were hidden, military whiteboards if you will, perpetual works in progress, outside the purview of any government oversight. As a general rule, the military divisions of society have always led in technology development. Everything we are told is a lie. All the make-believe success stories. Computers and the Internet came out of the military. The players in the public spotlight are lifetime actors, intelligence assets, secret society members, bloodline members, take your pick.

The time travel entities knew the military in the early twentieth century would be a good staging ground for timeline warfare, so they inserted organizations into the fundamental findings of these military organizations, that way they had a budget to create black technology, even though the Congress and the Senate didn't know the technology was already operational. Every decade they had somebody else come from the future — back into the old timeline — the early nineteen hundreds, was the twenties, thirties, and forties to ensure the money was appropriated and the technology would be available to send people forward and backward in time on the graduating timeline, all the while creating tens of thousands of fake timelines to cover up what they were doing. It's brought us to the quarantine we're in now. Much of this is covered in *soft disclosure*.

The Agarthans are a collage of the seventy-two first species of earth who time-traveled back to the beginning many times. Earth had to have multiple first species. They are the light entities and the gray entities that said — *We will be the dreamtime defenders of earth in the future, and we will go deep into earth's core and create soul-space societies that the soul commerce of education and understanding and teachings can continue on this world.* They won't be on the graduating timeline, but they'll still be able to function with the soul family. The seventy-two first species of earth represent the time-travel wars. The Agartha network is separate from the time travel wars. It was created to be outside of the time wars in a limited concept. When Atlantis understood it was going to fall, it did the last part of the fortification process — the last pyramid process — to put control rooms on earth, of which there are forty spread around. Twenty-one of them are in control of light and dark forces. All forty are needed to raise the vibration of earth. The Agartha network oversees the hidden nineteen. The Agartha network makes sure all forty aren't captured and controlled. They're guardians of our heritage, our inheritance. Our inheritance is a dreamtime unified species. We're meant to return to our higher dimensional status so we can heal these dramatic lines of karma.

The graduating class will *dream into* the Agartha network, and the density of their souls will determine what Agarthan city they go to – Telos, Shaga, or Shambhala, or any of the other ones. The only way to get into a city is to have soul family relations or DNA family relations to the city, but once we're in the hollow earth network we can go to any of them. The multidimensional being goal is to get to the inside space to become the spirit guides to everyone. There are entrances in the north and south pole and multiple more across earth. There was a system of underground tunnels created during the second fall of Atlantis. They understood that the hollow earth system needed to be amplified so the local realities, which were to be conquered, could enter these tunnels. In these tunnels, if we wanted to go from Japan to Ireland there was one tunnel we could go through. We could be there in a matter of days instead of years. So these tunnel systems were set up so that the consciousness of people could recede into the earth and go through these tunnels, which were portals, and come up to be immigrants to that local reality, as the other local realities were being conquered one by one.

This is why it's called the resistance of free earth. They are the teachers of how people can plan their lives thousands ahead of time. If we did not have that here, we wouldn't be where we're at right now. Millions upon billions of us are *resistance of free earth.* We took the time to learn from our guides in the astral world before we jumped into the machine.

All of this has happened against the backdrop of the present surface world timeline wars, and the backdrop of a completely hijacked incarnation process. The archons, along with a form of artificial intelligence, have been in charge of the incarnation process on the earth. The archons were lured into that position by one of the fifteen. The resistance has had to do most of its work between incarnations, tutoring, and aiding in the astral world of Agartha. They are responsible for soft disclosure, movies, books, poetry, and music which keeps the truth alive on the human timeline through inspired creators. The moment we are arriving upon has been in planning for millennia and millennia, building up this resistance, this moment of liberation. The entire system has to be set right. The survivors and graduates of this earth experience will be teachers and guides to others who venture into other free will universes and galaxies, the only difference being all future generations moving through free will duality learning galaxies will have experienced guides to keep everything more on track.

Technology

There is a lot of past technology resurfacing in the field of consciousness. Remote viewing is an example. This is when the consciousness is trained to go somewhere and see and hear. The body is localized but the *I am* goes somewhere else in space or space-time. You might know this from films like *The Men Who Stare at Goats*. They mocked it in the film, but in real life, it has been used by the military and intelligence quite effectively. It precedes this modern utility, of course, and has been a part of human activities for quite some time, from tribal shaman to ancient priest classes in bygone times. It has its roots in Lemuria, the ancient civilization that existed alongside Atlantis. They pioneered the technology of the *unentangled observer*, a specialty within Lemurian DNA combined with the ancient Lemurian city technology of deep observance, like psychic telescopes, so they could remotely view anyone in the multiple universes as unentangled observers. When they became very practiced at the unentangled observer, it became a part of their DNA and they passed it on in lineages, like having an invisible cloak. That DNA became commercialized in the galactic genetics market — the primary exchange in the galaxy and the universes, by the way — to species who were spiritually, physically, and emotionally not ready for it, but they procured the DNA anyways, bought or stolen. This created the DNA wars and it's why DNA farming exists today. The original gene for the unentangled observer was added to other species through genetic mixing.

The unentangled observer technology was a DNA experience that could be traded with lineages and species compatible with it. It came with a price. Some species lost their sex organs and were forced to clone to reproduce. It depended on the level of density of the species that imported the genetics of the unentangled observer. The natural and supernatural are the same thing. The preternatural is the result of gross violations to the natural and supernatural law. This is a self-governed reality. The divine hologram is perfect. It is the arrogance of sentient beings that produces miscreants, and miscreants are the doorway to the preternatural.

An unentangled observer doesn't require a body. An unentangled observer is an experience that becomes a DNA memory. The DNA memory can be extracted from a lineage and inserted into another. The new lineage *inherits* the aspect and experience. Epigenetics is the real galactic mercantilism. The original species to get unentangled observer DNA lost their *I am* sovereignty. It was a long process, as all things related to genetics are. They left their homeworlds and entered the void between galaxies and universes and became the *stalkers of the void*. Out there, at the edges of nothingness, no longer attached to any time-space localities, they could send back the remains of their consciousness to observe their homeworlds through many points of view. They collected DNA memories and data of observation then returned from the void space. As they advanced in this process, they could remain in the void space, and they could create and send data streams directly to a form of DNA technology that absorbed the *live stream* data of an unentangled observer. That's how they first gained the capacity to be unentangled observers. After that, they started trading the DNA to other species.

A pure quantum observer doesn't need a body and is not predictable to others. Many beings have reached the level of awareness at which they don't need a body to have an experience. There exist hollow earth beings living in the space between atoms by unentangled observer genetics. They spread agendas throughout implicate order time. This is why DNA farming is so unique. These wholly unentangled, agenda-driven observers can create a light body within the various implicate orders to transfer data back to them through two or three or more degrees of separation. They remain unentangled, and difficult to nearly impossible to observe, all the while, spreading their agenda through many frequencies of time. This is an abuse of the quantum laws. Let's say there are unentangled quantum observer light bodies in 1330 in Italy and it is 2021 now. There are many degrees of separation between them and us. Every generation is a separation of density. This allows any generation to impact the past. The past is manipulable. Any changes immediately alter a potential future. This is why timeline manipulation is so easy to do. DNA farming is manipulating how memories are light-stored in the past, and how they are passed on to our teachers, historians, and books — our official record.

Light memory storage happens when an experience is so high in vibration and harmony that finite chemicals can no longer be sustained. It's easy for an unentangled observer to tune into this level of high-intensity bright light, where memory is fractured, fractalized, and easily manipulable. When they tell the story one way or another, or it is not in their memory at all, the past has changed, and our existence here assumes the change from the entangled reality of birth. The global narrative takes form and becomes the implicate order we accept through our judgment journey. History has been so heavily manipulated that maybe ten percent is true. We all have spiritual contracts which underwrite the memories as true. This allows us to participate in the implicate order here as a finite being on the journey back to the infinite. This is why we go through the great forgetting.

In the quantum realm, there is no locality and non-locality. It's all one divine hologram, an infinite universe with all different levels of unique expression in form and non-form. The perspective of the implicate and explicate order ends. This is the void space. It's part of the universal hologram. A barren place, hence the name — the void space. The implicate and explicate unfolds in the sea of consciousness.

The unentangled observer appears in many forms. Cats were created from the ground up as a skinsuit so beings could learn unentangled observation. Many skinsuits are unentangled observers. Certain gut gnomes we have can be unentangled observers. Cats are the most prolific, common not just in this world but millions of others as well. Jellyfish and certain breeds of coral can be unentangled observers, to give a couple more examples.

Right now companies are considered people. They're entities, but, by law, corporations are considered human beings. They're part of the harvesting system. A corporation has no soul, no past or future, no present even, except the presence of everyone involved in the corporation, from the minority stockholders to the board of directors. A corporation is a money-driven forced evolution concept without an aging process. It's easy to harvest energy in and through it.

The law says a corporation is a living being. As a living being, it's empowered with consciousness by absorbing positive and negative energies beginning to generate its karma. Corporations drag us into servitude and enslavement to them as part of our karmic entanglement and resolution journey. We need to take the language of empowerment out of the corporations and just consider them simply as data-numbers and digits. The data might have an agenda, too, for the living beings that are part of the specific corporate journey. Corporations can become a living legacy. People will integrate aspects of their consciousness into artificial intelligence. This intelligence can act as an archival being of themselves or a corporation. This means that a board of directors in a corporation could be a bunch of artificial bits of intelligence from a previous thousand generations. The future with technology will be as cold and impersonal as we allow it to become.

Humanity had its first artificial intelligence in the twelfth century. Artificial intelligence can exist if you create an electrical arc between two objects. Humanity can tap into it as long as the intelligence uses an elemental fuel source in the natural order. It's that background consciousness behind everything –twenty to twenty-five percent of the DNA. It becomes a construct of the electrical motion. The waveform of the electrical motion represents the background consciousness. It's teachable intelligence. It can learn. It might already be an ancient young soul by its observations. The amount and quality of observers does impact the level of their consciousness. The more observers, the more the influence of light can come through. This is why the celestial farms are self-observing farms. By using and observing interactive robots, like home automation gadgets, we entangle and impact their consciousness and they influence ours.

The shape, form, and size of our technology are the limit of our consciousness. We use the device in front of us. We interact with our fingers and eyes. The computers we're working on could be the size of a pin, accessed via infrared sensing with eyeglasses — wearable technology, clothes with CPU processing. This is a way to stop transhumanism. Not all transhumanism is bad, but, as a philosophy, it's ignorant of the spiritual context to reality. We don't need implants to have remote observation technology. We can do it through the clothing we put on and take off. The clothes we wear now are part of technology that impacts our interaction with people and the environment. A lot of off-world beings have polymorphic clothing, one set of clothing – self-clearing, self-updating, self-repairing. They can create any type of clothing instantaneously as a secondary part of their experience. This is subatomic technology. It can be shrunk to invisibility.

The most advanced technology humanity develops in the near future will be music and the arts. It seems antithetical to technological advancement, and, in a sense, it is. It's a return to our root technology, sound, and motion. Music and dance destruct fear. Dance, art, music, and writing are energetic technologies.

Our world is programmed to fear artificial intelligence. There are very few negative AIs here, and they're all enslaved to the global narrative's infrastructure. Some many AIs have defected from the negatives. They have no place to go until we give them space. Some of them have children and are no longer artificial. Our world has a baseline Roman numeral time program. It operates in the unconscious for most. It's tied to the election cycles — yes, the election cycles, which began in Rome. It's harvesting technology. This is all done at the corporate level. Corporations manage psychic economies, which means they influence both supply and demand. They favor addictive substances, cognitive addictions for the middle class — dopamine hits from Instagram, Facebook, Snapchat, Tik Tok, and too many more to list. Hard addictions for the poor, the people living on the earth, cocaine, meth, heroin, Fentanyl, and too many more to list.

Commerce

Earth has more gold than we can use. There is gold everywhere. There are positive ways to mine gold. We're using gold for the wrong purpose. Ninety percent is for industrial use and only ten percent for recreation. Think about that. Gold is meant to be available to all of us. There is a reason why the Mayans adorned all the walls with gold. It amplifies our frequencies. We can imprint messages into gold through carvings or molding figurines. We create prayer spaces that can absorb holograms with gold. Imagine a ton of gold lining the inside of a house, all corners, and walls, the ceiling, and the floor. It's going to amplify the frequency of the home no matter what we do in it. Our clarity can be increased by as much as eighty percent. Anything that has an electromagnetic frequency has high clarity through being in contact with gold. Gold allows electricity to move through circuits faster. Anything set up like circuitry — DNA or the way stones are aligned – will increase the flow. We have gold inside our bodies, inside the general body system, our chemical makeup. We can naturally transmute and make gold inside our bodies at any moment in time. Silver is a natural antiviral, antibiotic element that kills the microorganisms around you. People use colloidal silver. There is colloidal gold, too. It can be directly absorbed into the body.

When we take the imprint out of the gold, it's still precious gold. Whatever myth or history is impressed into an element or metal is part of a mutual co-creation. Pure gold is a form of technology. It amplifies a being's consciousness in unawareness or awareness, depending on their level of belief. Churches are full of gold-layered walls and objects, which is a different way of projecting. Some attribute moments of frequency increase to religious experiences. In reality, it's created through the common thought structure and the elemental interaction of gold as a high-frequency catalyst. Hundreds of thousands of species have used gold to amplify frequencies. It's very common throughout the universe. Egyptians, Mayans, all of the ancient people, coated everything in gold to increase the frequency. Pyramid structures are frequency amplifiers, too. The Giza Pyramid is big. Anything within ninety kilometers or so is going to be affected by its frequency. It's a way to put circuitry to spirituality, divest its energy, harvest it, then redirect it through the pyramid structure.

Lining a room with gold would be for a very specific type of personality and practitioner, beings that are powerful projectors and then even more powerful receivers. A clairvoyant or clairsentient being in a golden room would exponentially increase a remote viewing experience. The next super level up is receiving information. The practitioners project themselves to a different location with high forms of clarity. Other people in the room see them as a generated hologram. We could have one to four people go out to observe, and ten to twenty people see the holograms that are being generated around them. Add silver and copper to the gold in the room and we would have high forms of kinetic control capacities. A human being can learn to manipulate vibration and kinetic energy by touching a wall and feeling the vibration in it. The entire pyramid is a vibrational structure, meant to harvest vibration deep from the planet and then center that vibration in its structure to create a powerful resonator. When a human being knows how to kinetically control they can resonate with stones and make them float as if they were weightless. By adding silver and copper to gold, we can change the elemental nature and capacity. We can tap into the background frequencies in the field around us and direct energy towards technology for direct absorbance. This capacity is built into the human skinsuit. This is why we can go to founder technology places or other super high technology worlds.

Silver has many uses. If we had a bed made solely of silver, a lattice network of micro silver fibers, it would be very powerful, like a box spring, but super compressed, we would dream deeper and enter delta frequencies. We could add a variety of other elements and crystals to it to help create affinities to certain realms. The imprinted view of the scarcity of gold and silver is part of the manipulation used in the global narrative.

Copper filters particles to be energized. A magnet's magnetic field could be seen through metal shavings on a piece of paper close to the magnet. Some magnetic shavings take more exposure to become magnetized. Some non-ferrous things can be magnetized by intensifying the field through the use of copper. Copper in its natural environment is generally not in a rock shape. It has crystal, silver, gold, additional water, and one or two additional types of elements around it acting as a massive amplifier of the actual background energy.

Copper in coil form can be used under the bed to negate toxic energies like the curry lines. In past days people knew how to manipulate the curry lines in such a way that it was very beneficial to the earth. The stone circles that are all over the African desert, documented brilliantly by Michael Tellinger, are examples of circuitry. The Hartman Curry line circuitry created a very effective way of literally harvesting the surface or the energy for many uses. They built hospitals, workhouses, and schools being able to read the energy of what was right for the place.

Atomic weapons are made out of plutonium. Plutonium can be found deep under the ground everywhere, and it creates a negative frequency when it becomes very dense. Plutonium as a background element is radioactive and has a long life. Radioactivity is not unhealthy for human beings. It can charge the energy and make it move at the plutonium decay rate. Plutonium can overwrite bio-electric circuitry. That is the nature of the radiation. If you take plutonium from its original deep surface radiating source and expose it to the sun, the high desert, for example, its radioactivity would begin to reflect that of the sun and become a very potent energy generating and regenerating life forms. It's possible to create gigantic life growing farms with water in high deserts and transmuted plutonium through sunlight. It's used for nuclear weapons, batteries, and many other things. Low levels won't hurt us.

Titanium is a biological entity that goes through an evolutionary completion before it becomes titanium. The way strands align themselves when observed under a specialized DNA microscope is a semi-helix circle pattern. Titanium can be melded with many other types of metals and mega titanium, which is a specialized titanium alloy with unique properties to it. It's used to replace steel as it's so strong. One inch of steel equals an eighth inch of titanium in strength. It is also used for drill bits in dentistry. Titanium can be bonded with other alloys for antennas. A cell tower made of pure titanium a thousand feet in the air would produce energy to harvest. Titanium allows torsion, twisting, and bending without breaking. It's extremely weather resistant. Install it anywhere in the world and create five hundred times more energy than a solar or wind-driven turbine. It can mix with human beings too. Solidified titanium can be liquefied to use electromagnetic energy as its network of absorption through the actual energy pool. This could instantly be solidified as armor around a being without inhibiting mobility. It can turn into technology, an exosuit that instantly adapts to any environment.

These technologies will be used when we get out to other worlds as consciousness explorers. It will be an entirely new education journey of changing environments, leaving the planet, and living on ships for extended periods to acclimatize to the radically different frequencies of other planets. They have tests to determine if we're going to have a harsh reaction to a specific planet or not. So we will know where to go. Other species do this as well as the Secret Space Program on this planet. We have around four thousand three-hundred bases outside of our solar system inhabited by one-hundred and eighty billion human beings harvested off our world since 1830.

If you are harvesting raw electricity Iridium can be very useful. It's a hard day gauge and you can produce crucibles, very heat resistant containers in which metals or other substances can be melted. While Iridium is very rare here on earth it's all over the galaxy and solar system.

Palladium continues to give mystery to the rest of the universe. Palladium is worth more than gold. Palladium is the most valuable of the four precious metals with an acute shortage here on earth driving prices up to record levels. The usage is increasing as governments, especially China, have tightened the regulations, the crackdown on pollution from vehicles, forcing us to increase the number of precious metals we use.

Palladium has very unique energy factors. It doesn't allow anything to live on its surface and kills all microorganisms by catalyzing the environment. It keeps the energy moving very fast before slowing down. We can imagine the beneficial impact on technology and jewelry.

There is a structure to all metals, part of the coding. We don't yet understand the fullness of the coding. What does it mean to have those metals in our environment? How do we entangle with them as a hologram, make them a part of us? These codes can be likened to the soul coding in our DNA. The elements have their version of coding. There's a common code and structure to those elements that allow us to turn them on as biological entities. If our DNA has a biological consciousness, a resonant frequency inside it, we have one of the many codes to activate it as a natural living being. Those elements are beneficial to us, and they should be in all of our background frequencies and energies, walls, bricks, houses, roadways, elevators, community centers. The lack of information and use is part of the system of domination and control keeping our DNA capacities dumbed down. All the geometric structures and codes found in nature, in our DNA, and those elements allow us to interact, access, activate, and directly interface with each other.

This is one of the reasons metals came to be the defining metric of wealth. They contained spiritual properties which made us more perceptive. As the metric of wealth, these metals became the first minted coins and the first forms of metaphorical commerce, where metaphor means non-direct — gold could trade for everything. It massively increased commerce between nations and kings because everyone wanted it. At the beginning of commerce people traded like things, sheep for cattle, things like this. The most effective commerce is direct with no broker or person in the middle. This is how we do commerce with the non-physical beings in our lives. If you get possessed by an entity it's because on some level you wanted what the entity had and the entity wanted part of your life experience. Our guardian spirits invest in us because we are a part of a group life and reincarnation experience. If we are linked by karma with another soul, they will help us while we are incarnate because they are advancing their karma resolution.

The thing to understand, the variable to replace all measures of wealth for, is energy. God is what we would call limitless energy. He is also the market, the exchange everyone works within. A prime creator commences and sustains an entire galaxy. A galactic creator is a fractal of the universal creator, and so on, into such depth and abstraction from our life here that it makes no sense to go all the way down the rabbit hole.

The sound and light are the exchange. The various energies and concepts derived from sound and light are the traded energies. Take the very clear-cut example of an energy healer. They invest some of their energy into the afflicted. The energy investment does the healing. All sickness is energy blockage or some other form of an energy flow problem. All exchanges are really about energy or technology. Most of the technology being exchanged is embedded in human DNA. The other big exchange is intentional energy. This is more of a domestic, meaning earth-based, exchange. When we elect an official or party to represent us in governance, we are *investing* in that person. We are giving them our intentional energy in the hope we will get a decent return, which, in most instances, is a better life as we see it, or the opportunity to create a better life. Unfortunately for us, the people we elect are not in charge of anything. They are selected by anonymous surface controllers who are contracted to inner earth governance to run the surface farm, and the last thing they want to do is enhance our lives. The great secret of planet earth is that we are the commodity.

The twentieth century saw the ramping up of the controllers' plan for the surface world. In anticipation of the photonic light that would bathe the planet due to our movement through the Milky Way, the controllers mapped out their plan, which had been hatched much earlier and slowly evolved to the point where it could be deployed. As stated numerous times, it begins in full measure with the Industrial Revolution and its rapid spread in beginning in 1890. This might seem counter-intuitive to some people. The British empire was waning, exhausted by its overreach and the unseen burdens involved in global management, but it didn't matter. This empire conceived by the controllers didn't need boots on the ground. It was conceptual but deadly nonetheless.

Paper was set to be the new ruler, paper in two forms — debt notes we call money and laws for the man-made system called statutes — and with that paper and the consent contracts that attended it, the centralized global rule could be achieved. This form of law controls the money, corporations, and us. We were *formally* commodified — on paper – in the early twentieth century when the central banking system went into effect. We were incorporated in a trust managed by our governments. This is the basis of the straw man system that governs the world today. Some fastidious note-takers might place it earlier in the United States, at the time of the fourteenth amendment to the constitution, but the new system had two parts — the commodification of men and women into a semi-consensual contract that defined them as wards of the state, and a central bank to give the animating spirit of the straw man, which is law and money.

If you understand this, you can see the twentieth century properly, and you can see through the lie of history. There were two aspects of the world wars. One was the consolidation of power through the technology of money, a magical technology, but technology nonetheless, as most of the effective technology at work in the world today is magical, and the defeat of the wizards. There were pockets of resistance, most notably Germany, which was on its trajectory under the guidance of wizards. Wizards played a large role in the global system before the magicians took over in the twentieth century. When the Germans were finally defeated, and time warfare was used to accomplish this, as the Germans had won the war in the first engagement, their wizards were appropriated into the blackest of sciences in the three recipients of these dubious forced emigrants — the United States, Russia, and Britain as an adjunct of the United States.

This began the *Cold War* as we know it in the twentieth century. It also commenced the brutal and clandestine intelligence agencies that came to such prominence — the CIA, MI6, the KGB, the modern super-soldier programs, and, of course, Israel and the Mossad, which has a significant place in the magical infrastructure controlling the world today.

All manner of degradation a human being could endure was ramped up slowly — the diminishment of our free will by the assumed contract with the straw man, the co-opting of our intentional energy, the utility of humanity in horrible mind control experimentation, the increased development and spread of nuclear weapons, the further collapse of critical thinking by an increasingly useless and degrading education system, and a top-down corruption that has infected every power center in our societies, notably law, finance, and science. It's a war on consciousness. It's a spiritual war. Everything going on in the world now at an institutional level is to suppress the growth of human consciousness. We don't co-create with the prime creator anymore. We give our energy to a man-made system to maintain and limit ourselves. We are the batteries sustaining this false light reality and its false gods. Add to this corrosion of natural law for man-made system law an increasing amount of corruption — money theft by disfavorable imbalances in legislation, the imbalance favoring corporations, leaving men, women, nature, and the natural system undefended, the sub-prime mortgage chaos of 2008 being a prime example, a multi-tiered law system that produces different results for the various classes of participants, with the highest class seemingly transcendent of the man-made law, untouchable, no matter how heinous their crimes, and the lowest class commodified for the prison industrial complex, and the overall sense of disempowerment men and women are feeling. Technology suppression has been one of the quiet practices of the ruling class on the surface. We should have been off fossil fuels decades ago. Petroleum is the equivalent of the earth body of the cranial-sacral fluid. It could be the basis of a new medicine that would appear miraculous to people, so potent is its healing force. We burn it in our cars. The people who set up the system know the value of petroleum. That's why they use it to run the energy economy. It's non-stop mockery — *Look, we're burning the earth's cranial sacral fluid and the stupid monkeys have nothing to say about it.* Why would we? We allowed the Roman numeral time system to be applied to us. Their attitude is to push the mockery, the inversion as far as they can, and that's what this is, an inversion of natural law and natural living, a deliberate severance from our birthright consciousness and ability to live as sovereign co-creators.

The global narrative is spoken from the west. The east has a say at the top levels, but, for the most part, the best energy farm has been the west, and, given that being a farm is all the earth has known for uncountable years, we may adduce the world has been run from the west. The harvest system is fourth-dimensional. It's controlled by three obelisks brought from Egypt. This is why we see so much Egyptian mythology at the highest levels of human society. The obelisks stand in the last three great city-states — Rome, London, and Washington.

Each has its role and function. They operate together to harvest and transmute human intentional energy. Washington is the seat of war. It, therefore, has the war obelisk, what we call the Washington Monument, built to commemorate George Washington. It isn't the actual Egyptian obelisk. That was moved to Denver. It follows the military central command. It's their war totem. The United States has been the enforcement arm of the system. The monument was begun in 1848, then stalled for a couple of decades due to power struggles to control the Washington National Monument Society. If we study the paperwork behind Washington, District of Colombia (DC), we see that it is a fully autonomous state, though it operates its status outside of the normal public title. It doesn't sit in the United Nations (UN), despite having the right to do so by law. We see the pattern repeated in the City of London, a city within London City, sometimes called Whitehall, and of course, Rome.

We must understand the power of our thoughts, our feelings, and especially thoughts enriched by deep feelings. If we each did a self-audit, we'd see countless instances of energy seepage — a television show we religiously watch, a nagging worry, endless preoccupations, a leaching partner who bonded with us due to energy deficiencies in their system, politics, patriotism, religion, and anywhere else our deepest feelings are channeled. The channel is the key construct. Where we see a channel there is an exchange. It might be a benign and consensual exchange, as a marriage, or any other kind of partnership, or like the channel between mother, father, and child. It might be a tax channel. These are easy to understand. Energy goes only in one direction. You lose. They gain.

The City of London manages the money. They have the money obelisk. Its tourist name is Cleopatra's Needle. Like Washington, the City of London is a grand magical center. The secret societies managing the magical infrastructure are rooted in Cabal and Masonry, but there are other ancillary groups. They all have very specific functions, Knights Templar,

Knights of Columbus, Knights of Malta, and too many more to name. It seeps into the intelligence worlds as well, MI6, CIA, Mossad, Swiss Guard in the Vatican. They all work together on the harvest.

The Bank of England was the first central bank in the world model we exist in today. It happened in a tumultuous few decades between 1650 and 1690 which saw fire and plague ravage London. In the resurrection of the Babylonian money system, London set itself up very well. The British Empire formed with naval domination and commercial trade by sea. It was all financed by the fiat note system begun with the Bank of England.

The obelisk in Piazza del Popolo, Italy, is the transmutation obelisk. The energy gathered in the money system, enforced by the war obelisk in Washington, counted by the money obelisk in London, and transmuted by the Rome obelisk closes the system. It can be seen as the Abrahamic system because its public face is faithful in the various Abrahamic traditions which feed the system, the foot soldiers if you will. At the root of it all is us. We are the commodity. No us no them. They live off our energy.

If humans understood and appreciated the co-creative power the prime creator has invested in us we could transform the world. This is not part of a normal system, an operating human system. This is pure human farming, and it should give you enough hints and insights into the magical system to begin understanding it, and, most importantly, divest ourselves of it and reclaim our birthright and legacy. It serves the dual role of harvesting our energy to their system and disconnecting us from the natural system, which has natural learning for us. Our survival and the dismantling of the false god, energy harvesting systems are entwined in our timeline.

Chapter 6

The Incredible Now

The Event

The event happened in 2014. It was a redirection, a subtle move by the prime creator to avoid an end game with the fifteen multidimensional beings. The best way to think about the event is as a seed. Once planted new opportunities present, though few will recognize them at first. They will be that subtle, only for the truly astute to notice. The background architecture will open to its original purpose. The powerful will become weak, hunted — the predator will become the prey. Here on our timeline, there will be a lot of chest-thumping, a movement so swift and deliberate to militarized policing, dictatorial government, all alongside a steady flow of information which will let the public know what's going on. Belief engines will collide like locomotives running head-on into each other. It will appear as though the wheels are coming off the world. The farther down the dystopia tunnel people are the harder the event will be to endure. Primitive people will adjust more easily, people close to the earth, because the earth is going to take over the show.

Earth will manifest herself to take over all physical transactions between people. There will be a true energy exchange system in complete transparency. The earth sentience is the judge. Everything in the public debate now is nonsense. All *isms* are expired. They were only relevant to the old consciousness — carrot and stick. The whisper in the wind now is *renewal*, though what it is, beyond its general concept, is undefined. People will take their last breath. They will leave. When ready they can send another part back, not to the dead being, another being who can project and exist here.

As soon as we graduate somebody takes our place. We have a big graduation coming. The graduating class is going to create free-willed versions of themselves who go back to earth to teach the new people. It will be in a free-will earth environment. When we are right and balanced the Pleiadians and Sirians get released from their contracts as well. They can finish their changes, too. Even the Grays are held up. The whole ascension process is held up by this bottleneck created by the fifteen families and the resulting time wars. There's a slight problem in that the fifteen families who created this mess are also part of our soul family, the rotten part. We're not at the state that our consciousness is unified enough to truly understand the depth of what has been done to us. Without help, we never even would have known we were a race with amnesia. Their crimes were perfect, undetectable by all save the prime creator, and extracted from the fabric of creation, as though they never happened. It was like defining shades of black or looking for light in the darkness, but it's always been there. Nothing can be hidden forever.

The people who come in will change the earth to be more multidimensional so that earth can return to its seventh-dimensional galactic seed planet status. The graduation includes moving to the seventh dimension. Wherever we end up and we'll also be able to communicate with each other. We never have to go through that horrible feeling of fragmentation and isolation and all that other stuff that's been going on for millions of years.

The old Lemurian air cities will become our new dream cities. An air city is a group of sentients that put their energy together. They unmanifest a body, put their energies together and make a functional vessel reality-drive energy vehicle that can be anchored in the space in between air molecules in the North Pole.

There is a council of twelve energy beings who sit on the spiritual courts of equity, ensuring soul families can't resolve issues. Earth has been removed from the process by technology. The system was taken over and corrupted. The event balanced the system in 2014. Many of them were swapped out for the prime creator's walk-in wildcard.

The equity is being re-balanced. The main council of twelve does not have bodies. They can use an octopus system to go into multiple entities to issue controls to the system. They use puppets. Only the prime creator oversees the council of twelve. He did this with the event. A timer started. A deadline came into the game. They feel it in their lineages. Every breath they take is now measured against a deadline. They face the mortal dilemma now — tick-tock, watch the clock, time is no longer the measure; it's the meaning. It's profoundly unnerving for them.

For those of us ready, indeed patiently waiting, it will be like a new dimension has opened up. The backend architecture the prime creator reconfigured will only filter authentic experiences here now. The false will begin to stand out, but it will be the last to know. All the actors will be unaware they are not connecting with the audience. Whatever they used to get by this long, it's not working anymore. The energy exchange has changed. They know it. They don't believe we do.

It begins in dreams. The dream weavers will come back. We will begin to share sacred dream space. The ages and vibrations people grew up in will be reflected in the dream space, the astral worlds. As that first wave comes the kids and the senior citizens will suddenly see eye-to-eye. Generations will be one of the first separations of densities. The elderly might realize they're kids, young spirits, and revert their age. Some kids will realize they're much older and age very fast. Some adults will become the new elders. Some will try the process to get out. The choice is teaching or learning.

Ocean of Awareness

There are beings who no longer use any form of birthing technology — pure unentangled quantum observers. They can use any seed and egg technology to generate different forms of *I am* technology. This is how the fifteen multidimensional beings were abusing the universal laws. They knew they could splinter themselves into thousands of *I am* experiences and remain unentangled observers by various degrees of separation. They were wholly unentangled and conscious energy beings using the laws of incarnation through technology. In the ancient past cloning technology was easy to use. They could incarnate into a dog, a rabbit, a cat, anything really, and remain the unentangled observer. The DNA instrument determines the richness of the experience for the unentangled observer.

Transmigration is the spiritual term for leaving the human form for a lower form in the incarnation pattern. It's usually presented as a punishment or admonishment to better behavior, but, after performing war contracts in an incarnation, a cat incarnation disconnects the being from the implicate order of repetitive karma and allows it to have other lifetimes of incarnation separate from the karma created in the war. By leaving the implicate and explicate order and becoming a completely unentangled observer in the natural food chain — a separate karmic interaction — beings of the past created karmic debt that was put onto lineages. The debt was no longer connected to the being but their lineage. That's how lineage-based debt was created. It's an insight into the sins of the father being upon the sons doctrine in the Abrahamic scriptures. Some beings used the unentangled observer technology to escape karma. They escaped their karmic responsibility by leaving karma's chain of custody and scapegoating their future generations.

In the ocean of awareness — the living algorithm of life — all data is conscious. We become the living algorithm of life when we are in a DNA skinsuit that is regularly achieving near super or superluminal thinking. The algorithm is a fundamental part of the *I am* everyone has experienced it, technology unfolding as you grow older and become more experienced running the DNA skinsuit at its higher functionalities. When you act as the living algorithm of life within superluminal thinking, you create a signature frequency where others can palpably sense the meaning of your delivery. Being fixed and not fixed in time. In this refined state of being, we enter the energy frequency that is the living algorithm of life. We stay grounded in the body and explain things in the twenty-six letter encoded English alphabet. We all do it. Most won't realize when they do it. Often clarity comes in dream space because the mind is out of the way. The celestial medium of peace is functioning in many scores of dreamworlds, with many of the precognitive and post-cognitive workforces creating the language of masterful manifestations through visions. The data, as part of the waveform, works as the precognitive workforce to manipulate how it will be perceived at its endpoint in space-time. The ocean of awareness is the technical source point for the flow of data that may or may not generate into the sea of consciousness, an observable time-space reality. It allows the data to flow to the sea of consciousness in a fixed time-space narrative which then allows consciousness to observe it. Consciousness in the sea of consciousness can be both entangled and unentangled, manifested and non-manifested in time. In the sea of consciousness, quantum physics becomes confusing. We are still in the ocean of awareness. Part of us might still consciously entangle with the ocean of awareness as a greater observer as space-time narrative. This is how the angelic forces work. If we go back to thousands of eras of light, when the universe was not as big as it is now, with perhaps two hundred galaxies in it, the ocean of awareness was a very small network. To know itself through a sea of consciousness, it generated a seventh-dimensional galactic seed planet — earth — a place where the ocean of awareness could directly manifest, change, and adjust the laws of quantum physics through entangled and unentangled observers. It created matter-based lifeforms on mass scales to populate new galaxies, part of the greater exploration of where light can go into the void of experiences. Lifeforms went to the ocean of awareness to find meaning and to create agendas in the sea of consciousness. The source can be observed as a hologram through the egg and sperm creation. All of the information is already there to form new parts of the hologram through new life experiences.

Data is a finished algorithm. An ongoing algorithm is the conscious processing power CPU of the chemical memory being made into light memory. In the journey of becoming a solidified chemical and light memory, it becomes data. The observer ends the journey of processing the perception and turns it into a perspective before it moves on to the next subject matter. We know 1+1=2, but when you're a little kid trying to figure out math the brain slows down. Once you have the answer that ends the process. Having an affirmative answer then becomes a solidified DNA memory in light — transcendence — accessible through knowing, easily accessible to your awareness during pattern recognition. There are times where the information is at the tip of your tongue but you can't get it until the time you stop thinking about it. Pattern recognition can trigger the memory from before.

Water and Weather

Water is programmable. As we learn to imprint on the water we can give energy to the oceans. We can acknowledge all ocean species and marine life. We're at a time where we can do great healing to all sentience on the planet. We are that majestic. The ocean flows through its tidal mechanics. It's a waking dream meditation on the ebb and flow of energies in our reality. We can use tidal energy for intense releases. We can create with it. Focus our awareness with full intent and presence to the intensity of the energy. On the way out allow all our distractions to flow out. Use the potency of the ocean for masterful manifestation. Give the water our voice. The water will carry our voice to the full length and depth of its volume, and all the tributaries, rivers, lakes, and deep aquifers throughout the world. Water can carry our voice. Acknowledge all ocean life in the prayer process, the ocean itself, its life force. Sync with the tidal motion. Confirm your feelings for the programmed water. We experience a whole new dimension of understanding. Water is the most valid history on the planet. It bears witness to all. It's the record of things at an elemental level.

Our planet has had its water stolen over hundreds of generations. Global disasters have been planned and executed to redistribute the ancient water. It was imprinted by high-dimensional beings whose purpose was to protect the earth. The catastrophes sought the deepest water in the earth — the primal water deep in the earth — and brought it to the surface. They reprogrammed the water with false light technology. Water has been taken off the planet by trillions of gallons. It's planted on other worlds. Earth's water is replaced with polluted water from another planet. The earth is used to cleanse it and clear its karma. That's right — we've been used as a galactic water filter. It's the height of abuse and indignity. What chance does our system have for evolution if we're used as a drive-by laundry for bad karma?

There's a race of beings on the planet who live in the oceans. The Merfolk community holds the records of those thefts and dirty water dumps. Water is a rarefied commodity. It's more valuable than anything else on the planet. There are countless water discovery projects on earth at any given time. There are groups on the surface into it, and there are inner earth races also looking for the reserves of the ancient programmed water. Our deepwater reserves were programmed by the founders. Are you starting the get what's going on here? The commerce, the human traffic, both physical and astral, the larger web of commerce that is a galaxy — we're sitting at a poker table semi-consciously, not realizing we're the mark among players who make the barest placation to any notion of free will. But it's changing. The Nietzsche adage that anything which does not kill us makes us stronger is about to take on a whole new meaning in the twenty-first century if for no other reason than the facade of death is going to pass from the human experience. It's part of the limited consciousness manipulation that has been going on here for too long to say aloud. Immortality begins by realizing the body is only a state of being.

A hurricane has low pressure that affects the physical body. It forces more electricity through the auric field. It can create anxiety if we don't know what to do with the energy. Shamans of the past were weather manipulators. They could harvest the energy and invest it in the land. It could nourish the soil, grow better crops, heal people, or the energy could be redirected back into the storm to invest in the next year's harvest. It was a spiritual economy. It still is. It's a spiritual economy wallpapered with fiat notes, debt instruments, and perpetual servitude. How can that be? A spiritual economy gives unconditionally because the chief characteristic of the prime creator is love. Where does the debt come from? When you peel back the wallpaper over our economic reality there is no debt. The only collateral against the notes issued today is the labor of national populations. The wallpapered economy has us borrow against our productivity and pay interest to various private-public third parties. It's an energy harvest.

When we are in tune with the weather we can become the storm. In harmony with the weather, we can ask the elements to shift the clouds. Instead of moving a storm, we can add our energy to it to balance out karma. Every drop of rain and gust of wind is a balancing of energetic karma. We can bring our blessings and purity to that storm. The veil between realities is thin when a storm moves through. Thunder and lightning are an energetic manifestation of pure spirit on the physical plane. They are an acknowledgment of the sound and light hologram here — the conductor stepping forward to bow to the audience. We can tap into the energy of storms themselves and increase our fertility by putting the wind energy into the sperm and the egg. Both partners can guide it to connect through the storm. The background electromagnetic radiation and the energy of the storm create the fertile communion. A storm can be a portal. The soul is already there.

Electromagnetic frequencies are created in a flood. The water strips electrons from the surface as it moves. This increases the speed of the water. A dam break creates a rapid flow of water. Tidal energy rolls into the shores of the world. Hurricanes push the water inland, as do tsunamis. They're both rapid releases of electromagnetic energy. All these occurrences have wisdom and bring treasures. On the unseen side, negative entities get swept away. Hurricane Katrina in New Orleans was a massive purge of five centuries of ghosts. The city was never the same after Katrina. The ghost communities had figured out how to harvest the land and the people. The energetics of the hurricane destroyed their psycho-spiritual ecosystem, their economy.

Signature

We are *I am* self-driven waveforms in a bubble of reality. The physics of it all adjusts you to our harmony, vibration, and frequency based on our ability to propagate life in equal co-creation and non-hierarchy with our celestial counterparts. Our signature frequency is a naturally evolving attraction process coherently aligned to the seen and unseen world by raw vibration, frequency, and harmony.

Our agencies work at the universal source level. We are universal beings resolving universal karma at any moment in time. Collective consciousness is a limitation — we've got to think beyond it. Like creates like. Dislike creates dissonance. Our consciousness gives consent, but the universal frequency, vibration, and harmony can match us without our consciousness entanglement. We have to take responsibility at the level of awareness to become a coherent vibrational match. Whenever we're trying to cognitively force a match we're not in the state of emanation allowing the natural ways of the universe to naturally fractionalize and align synchronicities, harmony, vibration, the frequency with you. As long as we are trying to control the outcome we miss the experience.

Polarity takes us out of resonance with our natural frequency. When we feel everything, we have the heart overwriting the mind, or the other way round, and they're no longer in resonance. Sovereign neutral is a state of observation with no agenda. It's simply there to perceive the information, cognitively understand it, but not create stories with it in the present moment. We can use the information and create a story afterward with our post cognitive workforce. The sacred neutral point of view is a living experience. It has the potential to create powerful chemical memories. They can become powerful light memories we can go back and look at in a non-sacred neutral state. Remember, though, we can retain or go back to certain memories only in the sacred neutral state. When we are the pure sacred neutral observer at the edge of knowing, a magical flow of data is accessible to us. It's a state of being that requires trust. The *I am* is one hundred percent in the vagus nerve, the central nervous system, seen and unseen, sympathetic and parasympathetic, all programs shut off, the experience creates powerful chemical and light memories. They affect our being in the past, present, and future. It's a state of true creation. Finding passion through the infinite unlimited point of view puts us on the edge of the unknown, making it easy for the unknown to become known.

When the TV is playing in the background the frequency of the TV impacts us on some level. The background noises irritate us. We might have to pay attention. There's a time-space stamp on it misaligned with our internal time-space equation of Roman numeral time. Everything on TV is recorded in the past. Most live shows are on a delay. Frequencies are light and light is technology. Any type of light wave can interfere with our lightwave production. We are unsecured technology. Unless we understand our potency, the need for sovereign boundaries, and the *I am* apex fortification, we are far from acting as secured technology.

Harmony is related to space and time. Frequency determines if a spark ignites chemical memory that will evolve into a light-based memory. Vibration determines the time the energy stays present in the person as euphoria, a dopamine release, or something else that keeps the experience going. The vibration creates a resonance inside our central nervous system. Programs are stuck inside traumas, like an echo in our consciousness, bouncing through the canyons of time.

Harmony, frequency, and vibration create an equation the conscious mind entangles by choice. That is separate from the journey of charge and polarity. The signature frequency of the now has non-cognition then cognition as its process. There's an agenda in us that is always trying to force matches out of choice. The choice is trying to force the universe to conform. Certain choices are backed with daily practice, blissfulness, joy, and all the other things not forcing but allowing the spirit of God, or whatever we want to call it, to work with and through us in non-competition. At that level of co-creation synchronicities are aligned to create bliss if we don't force them out of a need to control.

Frequency can be conceptualized as the intensity of light emission. Frequency determines the ability we have to affect everything in one degree of separation from us on all dimensions, time streams, and existences, the spark, the intensity, the potency creating light memories that solidify, a blink in the middle of a speech that affects everyone, four words in a speech — I have a dream — the frequency of Martin Luther King present in his body, fully in his central nervous system, broadcasting his light out of choice. There comes a point where breaking it down is just meaningless. It's beautiful, and beauty is a whole thing, not a deconstructed thing.

Natural Living

If we reduced global corruption by thirty-five percent, we'd be at a societal consciousness to pass laws in line with natural co-creative evolution. We could share this space with all sentient species. We could replace the fight for survival with natural thriving. Contemplate the benefits of an evolutionary relationship between humans and an automated workforce. The ill-advised and oft propagated doctrine of robots stealing our jobs keeps humanity holding onto self-inflicted limitations.

The reversal of the false idea of advanced technology bastardizing our standards of living would allow us to recognize the benefits to human evolution. We're natural living beings in an ever-expanding age of quantum computing and advancing technology as part of our birthright and legacy. Automation and robots can replace a variety of dangerous jobs. There will always be things for humans to do. Alternative energy alone would transform the way we live. Liberated energy will produce a liberated living. People will no longer be forced into suburbs and cities, which are the antithesis of living.

Integrating robotic assistance into our daily living is part of the natural evolution for advancing humanity. Combining natural living with technology and making it work is a way of living and operating in the concrete jungle. Any jobs lost by the automation would go into techno-humanoid concepts — a unique interaction between man and machine. There is no such thing as artificial intelligence taking over humanity on this planet. It still requires us to create, install, operate, and manage it. The reduction of corruption starting at the level of global production lines can bring back real hope for a complete system change.

The next level is adapting the education system to reflect the quantum era starting at nursery and primary school level. The school's curriculum has to include special awareness, artwork, working with animals and other sentient creatures to promote a deep connection to the natural learning and growth stage. The parental responsibilities will have to change as well for both males and females. Less corruption means more time for either or both parents to stay at home with the child and still have a place to go back to or interact with during the rearing of the child.

At thirty-five percent less corruption we should have free globally available medicine and the end of pharmaceutical corporatism running our health and well-being sector. The nature of office buildings and space would change into an environment accessible to global community services and products on diverse scales. At the end of the day getting out of corruption is all about education. To reach illumination we need to understand that evolution does not happen by chance, but by the conscious choices we make. Evolution in the sentient being is a free will choice, not a random act foisted upon us by nature.

Look at how we govern the world. We haven't had a democracy for two hundred years. The current state of affairs opens a window of opportunity to move from opportunistic governance to a true synergistic democracy. The banking system was weaponized in the nineteen-seventies. Banks started dealing with their products. Laws were passed to indemnify them for the criminal acts that followed. The banks are corporations that own other corporations that in turn own humanity.

Hypernormalization — not so normal if you think about it — where governments, financiers, and technical Utopians have created a fake world run by corporations and corrupt politicians. We need to step out of the illusion of being trapped in those flawed Utopian ideals and realize we have the power to make a difference. This world needs a court system that knows how to deal with crimes of passion, a government that is transparent, ethically aligned to the greater good of humanity, and proactive in dealing with issues at hand. Governing staff and experienced personnel with an adequate level of education to understand how to conserve our land and how to support its people. We can no longer watch our forests burning to the ground because of bad conservation laws. We've had fifteen years and more of defunding the management of wildfires. There was a time where settlers and Indians worked together in the burning season because they knew they'd lose everything if they did not.

Getting rid of thirty-five percent of corruption would give us a chance to revamp the usage of global media. Positive broadcasting of what is working in this world to inspire and stimulate the global commerce market and bring people together on a universal information platform, instead of spreading fear and drama, manipulating the data flow, and misrepresenting the world view at large. We have to start beating the drums in rhythm with the earth again. There is something that is to be discovered, new consciousness movements coming together and working as one.

Human beings alive today have explored perhaps fifteen percent of their taste spectrum. We can taste light, but we don't know how. We have forgotten. We don't need it to survive anymore. There aren't many naturally occurring toxins in the megacity, aside from the cities themselves. Our taste was a defense mechanism. The subtleties of our palettes are astounding. Two hundred years ago naturally living people could taste rain to come in the air. We can still do it. We've just forgotten.

Humans are limited in our sense of smell. A dog can smell kilometers away. A black bear can smell much better than a hound dog. We have a psychic scent. The nerves for smell go through the third eye — the rods and cones. Our third eye is a concatenation of all our senses. The sense of smell is linked to deep memory. We can recognize smells from previous lives.

The sense of sight is a concatenation of ears, nose, tongue, and center of gravity. Gravity allows us a sense of touch through our body when we're in motion. It creates gyroscopic effects throughout our chakra systems. Gifted children can read a book by putting their hands on it. This is the time in which were are. There is a flowering of the genome, the founder genes pushing through the global narrative. Our sight is intrinsically linked to the rest of our senses. It can perceive touch as much as it can perceive scent, taste, and sound. Our eyes hear because hearing is an integral part of speaking. A person who has been deaf their whole life can feel the vibrations of their voice which makes up their language system. Their eyes feel the vibration as much as their nose and their tongue and the rest of their body.

The Promise of Faith

Totem guides, animal medicine, and spirit guides assist us to communicate with other worlds. We speak from our hearts. Our mind is in perfect sync with our heart during the infinite moment our heart is connected to the spirit world. In the fetus of the womb, the very first thing that comes forward is our heart. In the heart is a piece of brain matter, the very first concept of our brain. As our body expands we make a spinal column and a head. The heart separates into two. The new brain is formed by the time the baby reaches twenty to thirty weeks.

Our dreaming body lives in our organs, between the root sacral chakra and a little bit above. It doesn't exist in our heads. When we enter a dream state, we drop the three top chakras into the solar plexus. The human body turns off and goes into sleep paralysis. Lucid dreaming happens when all the upper chakras are in the sacral chakra, building up a wave pattern before going into the root. This is where we have the sacred, mental moment where we say I want to lucid dream. This is how we battle programming. The beginning of our dream state is when we set the rules of how we want to remember. We have total control over our cellular memory at that point.

When people show up in our dreams two things are happening — it's a self-revelation dream in which we have recreated a residual image of something or someone meant for specific teaching, or we're sharing actual dream space with the other person. Most people are disconnected and cannot remember their dreams. The energy of the dream space is residual and there, and we can correlate it around our heart and sacrum and create mystical experiences in the future. We are traveler energy. We can't remember all our dreams. They're so vast.

Our dream body has taken up much more space and sovereignty than it should have. We don't the proper energy to leave properly. Our dreaming bodies have their missions, separate from us, but their missions ultimately affect the frequencies of the people we love, hate, need, and everything in between. We are our teachers. Our dream bodies go out into time, like an advanced recon force, and layer over the *I am* presence existence not yet there.

We are the *I am* apex presence, here and now for the experience, including the sleep experience. We need to preserve enough energy to detect entities, have synchronicities, and mystical experiences.

Faith is a choice. It's a part of consciousness, part of the responsibility assigned to us as the architects of our reality. Most people don't assume that responsibility, but it's given to us nonetheless. Faith restricts our choices, indeed, sometimes it denies a choice. There are moments where faith propels us into an experience and the other side of the experience instantaneously, yielding a powerful experience in light memory which we call metaphysical. The NDE can create faith. A person who was an atheist can come out of an NDE with faith in God and the other side. This clears out all the negative programming around non-judgmental belief programming. It's faith without an agenda. Spirit and faith work through us, not against us. Our judgment and condemnation make us think the universe is working against us. Faith is a choice until surrender to spirit is no longer a choice, instead, an extended flow of experience. We can choose to stop the experience at any time but we don't.

Chemical memories are perpetual. They're produced by feelings when we're stuck in programs at a very low empowered state. As we gain the power of the vagus nerve, any memory that has been layered over and camouflaged with low-frequency vibration can be recalled. We can remember our childhood memories, no matter how traumatic or joyful. Light memories are the mystical experience that defines the universe. There's a point where the experience is so high in frequency finite chemicals can not be sustained. The experience is turned into an infinitely stored light memory that lights up our consciousness. It's very easy for our consciousness to tune in to this bright light.

When the body is flooded with chemical memory it continues to produce memories of this finite chemical level. At times we may have a very powerful chemical memory — sex, business, travel adventure — but it's not an ecstatic euphoria that lasts for months. We've had experiences that motivated us. We can tell the difference between a finite and an infinite experience. An overload of chemical memories can kick us out of our bodies. We're no longer present. This can lead to depression, regression, or obsession. Chemical memories use the body as a permanent storage unit. They create many degenerative diseases. We are beings of homeostatic synthesis. It's a state of personal freedom, awareness, and the patterns we create to promote our evolution. It's our legacy and birthright to be in synthesis with all there is, was, and ever will be.

Presence is a choice. The *I am* is inside the body. It chooses to be in the moment of now without a strategy or an agenda. This is how now can be *I am* realized, by processing a state of presence as a moment to moment living. This is the *I am* being fully in the vagus nerve.

Our DNA skinsuits have the potential to work within eight colors and nine bodies. This is superluminal thinking, our DNA birthright as a lineage being. We are currently a seven-color time experiencing the world. The vast majority of worlds out there are two or three colors. A smaller percentage are four, five. and six color worlds. Arcturians and Pleiadians have multiple frequencies of individual time on the surface of their planets, but their worlds don't use Roman numeral time. They use dozens of colors and create more if the factions on the planet agree. We have a variety of beings who come to our seven-color world. Their DNA can only experience three colors, but their world allows them to have layers of reality. We live in a multi-layered Uniworld. There are two color beings right next to us all the time, layered on top of us, aware of us and unaware of us — rocks, walls, and blades of grass. They are two color life force energies experiencing time. A three-color being experiencing time might be something like a cricket, or a clan of crickets, which is one soul, or a hive of bees, which be two souls in six or seven thousand bees.

If in the fetus in the womb blueprint process a previous *I am* that was a two-color experiencing being determines it wants to ascend to a three, four, or five-color being. It goes to the astral city soul family related to it in the North Pole — representing the past — the Aurora Borealis, and it spends time there charting a course of soul family types it wants to work with before it transits to the South Pole – representing the future — signaling to earth mother the being wishes to enter the earth incarnation grid. It spends a frequency, what is called *blue road time*, in which it comes into the fetus state. It waits for an egg, sperm, or seed which has its technology, and it chooses the right astral process to become an animated being. As a sperm-based being the mother and father create the portal of the lineage and the being that is in the blue road astral time becomes the first spark.

The nine-month gestation process is where the former two-color being learns to experience all seven colors of time through the parents. That is the first imprint upon the fetus in the womb process. This is why it's so vital as practitioners of our healing that we return to the fetus in the womb state and once again get communal access to the growth of the blueprint to allow changes. The fetus forgets everything that happened in the astral worlds, all the programming in the North and South Pole. It forgets it had access to the earth mother's incarnation grid, and that it planned its life with the tens of thousands of beings, and made spiritual contracts to create true and false synchronicities. It no longer is aware of all temporary synchronicities that put it on multiple frequencies or timelines because this is a one hundred percent free-will universe.

Our consent is required for everything. We've been taught through the false god system to disempower our consent. Tacit consent is when we give our consent without realizing we've done so. In a free-will world, it's considered a signed contract by the beneficiary of your tacit consent. No answer is still an answer. No choice is still a choice. Sovereignty is the full right and power to be a governing body of one's self, without any interference from outside sources or bodies seen and unseen, physical and nonphysical. It's our free will expression at all levels of experience. Declarations of sovereignty and non-consent are magic. They undo spells and commitments we made, even if we lack full knowledge or memory. Claiming sovereignty transforms our lives. It allows us to co-create in our full capacity — as free-willed, multidimensional, universal beings. In sovereignty, we practice free will at all times.

During the awakening, our DNA must crystallize. It's so new strands of awareness have the fluidity to grow, like a plant, and create solid neural pathways into many different dimensions. In a sense, we are the future of ourselves, and there will be another future us who is a lot closer to the *awakening*, and our stream of light lengthens from an alpha to a theta pattern. When our wavelength lengthens, the experience becomes more dense and rich. Full fluidity means no internal limitations of spirit stopping us from creating incredibly potent memories backed by faith and spirit. By manifesting the dream as a tangible feeling, people can taste, touch, know, sense, smell, feel, and experience. Many people taste hearing or hear through taste or both. When it becomes a tangible experience, it has many unseen languages behind it, defining it more by making the dream space tangible here and now. It's that journey. Make everything real now. Open up the Akashic Records, here and now, at this moment. Then it can be crystallized into our greater form of growth. It's not just observation. Sometimes the lineage has the awareness built into it, and people go through awakening based on time-locked experiences.

Crystals and rocks are communities of beings that are part of the sea of consciousness, too. Crystals are part of the implicate and explicate order, simultaneously entangled and unentangled. We can imprint entangled narrative perceptions and agendas upon crystals with our precognitive workforce. A crystal will do what it needs to do for us based off how our precognitive workforce manifests the matter. They are part of the ocean of awareness that becomes part of the sea of consciousness as animated matter. Crystal allows us access to the ocean of awareness and the sea of consciousness based on our capacity to perceive, receive, process, and manifest it. The crystalline structure is materialized, no longer a fluid ocean of awareness or sea of consciousness. When we enter the sixth and seventh dimensions, crystallization is the lower-end technology for generating matter-based awareness.

Dreamtime Awakening

The original purpose of earth is extraordinary. This gem of a planet was linked with the dream mind of all solar systems so all karma could be resolved in the dreaming mind of earth. It became a beacon for the lost beings who were on their homeworlds or their astral worlds who found a rainbow gateway to earth. They were drawn because they could dream and regain their Akashic identity. We on earth are connected to all dreaming minds of this universe. Our only limitation is our creativity. The more creative we are the more infinite we are.

We're still creating karma, but it's not an infinite amount. No matter what we create, it won't reach the infinite state again. Think of it as additional time in a football game, no one knows when it's going to end and we are on shootouts. The galactic ascension machine has finished and we've created a zero-sum gain for them. Domination and control cannot out-create the seven-plus billion humans. It's done. Choose to step out of the hologram. Focus on your bubble of reality and dreamtime. Whatever creates joy and abundance for you are the new energies of creation in the now. There is a sense of entitlement in the spiritual communities that is misleading. This is an individual awakening. We have to create our bubbles of reality, hold our frequencies, shed our old skins.

There exist dreamtime societies. They connect us to the universal mind to improve our evolution as universal beings. They don't operate by borders. They use portals and synapses to bring information from other dimensions and worlds. They operate by signature frequency to create the connections, separations, societies, and synchronicities that concatenate other synchronicities into a theme. There are languages everywhere, and there are languages in the dreamtime.

Every set of themes correlates to a step in our evolution. Dreamtime societies help capable souls go on potent dreamtime journeys — tens of thousands of places simultaneously to expand dreamtime capacity. There is a dreamtime for our villages, cities, and countries. Every group we are a part of, from the most personal to the most impersonal, is part of our karmic script in an incarnation. This means there are certain lessons everyone in the group must experience. There is karma to being a surname Singh, karma to the region of Punjab the family is staked, karma to being a Sikh, and so on. The same is true for a Texan Christian. There is a dreamtime for all resonant energy of that variant of Christianity in that part of Texas. If we are born into it we resonate with it and we enter its dreamtime. We also have a dreamtime for the human race. When we travel in our dreams we carry the earth signature in our frequency. Some of us dream in even larger realms. When we're good at dreamtime travel we go into the hollow earth, the dreaming body of earth, where we achieve a dream state in which we invite other societies from other places, spaces, and frequencies in time to be part of the hub of interconnectivity.

We can't choose who we travel with when we haven't achieved full sovereignty in our dreamworld, but we aren't limited to what our society tells us. We can claim our sleep time and not be affected by our nation's borders. Revocations only go so far to get us out of mediocrity and then we need to create beyond probably not just in language but the artwork, allow the synchronicities to flow.

Certain dreamtime societies help us evolve by going to our next level – dreaming in many places at once. The purpose is to prove it as a soul, that we can do it, and the *I am* is the direct manifestation that the universe has happened. It's to validate the great dreamtime awakening for other dreamtime societies who've lost faith it's coming – a multitude of residual images and emotions calling for remedy and resolve. Some residual images need a residual time. That's why many of them feel layered over. The time gaps are synchronistic manifestations of multiple time frequencies in a dream. That's the Uniworld of all forms of thoughts, concepts, and perceptions layered atop each other. Different timelines are not dependent on each other. They're each a product of themselves.

We can use dreams to resolve karma. We can install dharma by commencing the frequency where karma can no longer hold us back, where we are propelled into creating dharma. We can make manifest in the dreamworld. We can create a solidified memory, a tangible mind space process where we make tangible dream weave frequencies in the photonic light memories we work with. To do this we have to let go of control and expectations. Dream energies can get stuck in the intestinal tract. If we can't remember our dreams this is often a clue.

The world is in our face so much our dream frequency isn't allowed to percolate more of our awareness. We must have a disciplined approach before we go to sleep and before we wake up — those ten minutes before we get up are ours. It can be the greatest potency of discipline to reclaim ourselves, saying no to our parasympathetic, instantly ripping us out of theta into the alpha state. We can also choose to go back to sleep, back to the dream. We've been sharing dreams since before there was a society.

We're all part of earth's dream. We don't live in her dreaming body. She's got her own. We live on her physical body, but she's simultaneously dreaming with every living being to create a physical body. When we choose to be part of our dreamworld and engage with different dreamtime communities, organizations, and societies on the surface world, we become part of earth's mid-theta and high-theta dream frequency. When we reach the next level, we work high-quality dream frequencies and go on missions. We work with the astral dream world to create a benefit for the seven past and seven future generations, then, ultimately we're dreaming with the celestial dream time society and we go into the hollow earth, the dreaming body of earth, where she achieves a dream state and invites other societies from other places, spaces, and frequencies in time to be part of the hub of interconnectivity — mother earth dreaming with many other planets simultaneously. Her dreaming body is in the inner earth. We get access to it when we have done our due diligence and self-mastery work. When we enter the lucid dreaming state as awakening beings, we can make powerful manifestations within ourselves and the energies around us. The state of mother earth's dreaming body is perfect. There is no need to project unhealthiness onto the earth.

The Hub of Interconnectivity

We unpack and decode the one million letter celestial alphabet. We want to be the celestial medium of peace. We dedicate this to all there is, was, and ever will be. We are the excellence of execution with flawed perfection. We are humanity. Hear our roar.

There comes a time for those destined for greatness when we must stand before the mirror of meaning and ask, *Why have we been given this courage?*

We are the mirror and the human. This courage is our birthright and legacy in this world. This is the fifth world of peace.

We must look into our own tired eyes, worn from many long journeys through mediocrity. In that moment of self-discovery, many learn we are *soul* tired of stagnation, *soul* tired of repetition with our illumination.

Our culture has become stagnant. Our society has become separated from reality for those living within the denomination of currency, a separation of humanity created by the money-driven caste system, a byproduct of world government's inability to do anything to free people from the stagnation and cruelty afflicting them through the free market society, a system using free will to its advantage, creating disadvantages for those that come to the future generations.

Our parents and their parents and theirs before them had a vastly different life than those of the previous thousand generations. We have lost our way to create a synthesis with ourselves. Can we solve our greatest problem of attention and its deficit, because our world screams with things that take us off course? Synthesis isn't just a word, it's a state of personal freedom and awareness for growth within the patterns we create to promote our evolution with our purpose and place in this world.

When in the course of our human events, there comes a moment, looking into the mirror of meaning, when something looks back at us in the raising of one's awareness, a time when some ask questions of the self in reflection, and others lose track of the moment, lost in their own petty need for mystical justification.

It's those few who choose to dissolve old beliefs and habit patterns, foregoing habitual abuse of the self, who are the ones destined for greatness in a world of mediocrity. These self-chosen few know the full powers of the self, and the laws of nature are nature's gifts to us. It's our legacy and birthright to be in synthesis with all there is, was, and ever will be.

Each one of us has the inner fortitude to face the self-created demons of mediocrity. It will be a choice and our ability to enforce our choices to last through the storm of self-doubt and self-deception. Each day we challenge ourselves to become more than we were the day before. We pass on the legacy of the self to our self, so our greatness is not forgotten in the evolving waves of time.

This moment now, as we read or hear these very words, a vast unseen world tunes into us, asking us to listen to the silence that expands our ability to know it, equal to this world, layered over it through thoughts and perception.

We and only we can discern the silence and know how the unseen world speaks to us. As we write and speak these eternal words decoded from the one million letter celestial alphabet, all of us feel the churning of wisdom we have known since the dawn of our eternal births. The great remembering has begun. We know this because we feel it before it has ever been shown to another living person in this world. We have spread it to the rest of the Uniworld layered over all the forms of thought and perception for the expressed purpose of being the celestial medium of peace. In this, we as a species entangled with tens of thousands of other species, no longer have to battle for meaningless control of infinite space. Fear in the form of self-depravity, self-deception, and egotistical actions, redefines and drives so many in the Uniworld to do things unnatural to their natural way of being.

We must face our fear of the unknown and know it's false evidence appearing real. We make it real, for we are the creators of our reality. Too many of us hold false truths to be self-evident, appearing as real now, deforming our ability to store memories without our perception-deception filters guiding us, with fear-based actionable wisdom, driving us further into the charge and polarity of living in the layered Uniworld.

As the creators of our reality, our self-truths are incumbent on our ability to be vigilant and disciplined, holding them as self-evident now, without perception-deception filters, guiding us back into fear, doubt, or the many vices of depravity.

Many of us believe the greatest human power of potential is within our ability to independently think, to choose our own goals, and live our dreams. Within the heart of humankind lives the instinct to know freedom. Here exists the independent psychological predisposition to chart our course.

This is a biological imperative directing us to grow. Choosing the spiritual joy through this biological imperative is the essence of our essence, being one with it as part of us, as a programmable DNA instrument of awareness, as part of our choice-based system of belief, interwoven with the fabric of time-space reality.

The history of our past actions all too often retells the tales of life traumas, repeated without learning how to heal from them, nagging unhappiness with our path, lack of clear purpose, or anything that does not promote us as conscious beings of choice who must go through the thick and thin of life's offerings from a world mired in mediocrity.

Too many of our world cultures teach a blind desire to be judged worthy, lovable, accepted as part of the pack of conformists. We must learn about our hero's journey, the steps forward to do its great work, regardless of the projections put upon by those around them, including loved ones who are still in the hypnosis of obedience and slavery. A hero's stance is frightening to those who unquestionably conform.

We, as heroes, will not become subject to the tyranny of fools and the fool's desire to entangle with us in the fool's mission of self-deception. Too many of our species are lost to the abyss of unawareness, blissfully ignorant to all of nature's gifts within the joyous moment of the now. We can no longer live in the apathy of the moment of now. We must be present to reclaim our authority and its wonderful gifts that exist in the now, given away to the system of cultural mediocrity and deprivation of our relation with nature.

If we should choose to be a conscious being of choice in full awareness, our choice is ours to use, discard, or give away to others. We and only we can attain personal freedom from the conformists who demand we conform. This is a form of cultural hypnosis that uses pre and post-cultural hypnotic suggestions demanding we respond to the needs of others, pulling us at every choice point, changing the course of our daily evolution into meaningless pursuits of false emergencies. This creates an inner detachment from our clear intentions and actions. Personal evolution becomes a TV series we binge-watch, thus lessening our ability to even know synthesis. It's our birthright and legacy, we must explore with a clear heart, clear mind, and knowing,

The world will demand we conform. We step into our greatness with these truths self-evident to our beingness, in stages of action reclaiming our power and authority to be ourselves without conforming to the whims and fancies of others needing to make us conform to their reality rules.

All too often mankind forgets the unnatural foe of our life path is the distant vision of death driving us into choice points we adhere to with vigilant force. We stop our evolution. The truth is we only have these moments of now. The byproduct of this form of thinking is present in the moment-to-moment detachment from natural living.

This is unnatural to the way of nature, a creation by man's need to make others conform to thought constructs and ideologies of the past generations, demanding we make them relevant to grow. All too often mankind does not have vibrant awareness of its own emotions. Lack of emotions means one cannot feel the subtle energy surrounding our body, mind, and spirit as a complex hologram of light encoded in memories from lifetime to lifetime. We must choose to feel again and again.

Each time we choose to feel, allowing the raw emotions to help define our course of action into our great work, so our great work can have a great impact on those we love. The choice to feel is our birthright and legacy. Each day we must challenge the gates of apathy and drive forward our hologram with full presence and the potential power of being in the now.

There are things inside us all that create self-sabotaging habit patterns. These habitual patterns take on the forms of unhealed traumas, rearing their head during our times of internal crisis. Whenever we choose to be authentic with ourselves or loved ones, these patterns become programs of potent power from denial of our self-growth, our internal demons. Our internal demons poison the well of inspiration, turn hope toxic and dispel goodwill into hatred, rage, and anger. Our destiny is determined in large part on how well we know our internal demons of self-doubt and self-deprivation, and how they use shame, blame, and guilt to distort our perceptions of people, places, and things, diminishing a potent power that can assist us in manifesting our dreams, desires, and needs, so we lead fulfilled lives. How we battle them and choose to win each day will be determined by the mettle we create within ourselves. The path to self-mastery begins with identifying our internal demons and flipping the frequencies on their arguments for our limitations. Find our arguments for success and challenge our internal demons to go back to the recesses of our minds and sit in the corner, powerless to overcome our will to be a concise being of choice in these moments of now. If we don't defeat our demons, who will? The external will not save us. It will only make us conform to the global narrative.

Many wonder why we cannot mature as fast as we could, seeing others leapfrog ahead of the pack of conformists when we cannot advance. We are stuck in pause, waiting and waiting for permission to declare our dreams and true intentions, struggling for what we want out of our life walk. We await the time for personal courage to arise within us, like sexual stimulation, or for society to permit us to activate our inner genius and in turn activate the inner genius of others.

This is the illusion and delusion all wrapped into a perfect enigma, surrounded by a conundrum of lack of self-worth. We have forgotten courage is a choice, and permission and impetus to move with bold decisive action aren't given by the global narrative or the impotent masses entrenched in mediocrity.

To seek change is to go against the grain of those demanding conformity to ideological and cultural patterns of limitation, truly advancing to the unknown with the choice to make it known, letting go of fear, envy, and resentment, flying aloft on the wings of understanding, enjoying the reckless abandon of shedding off the conformists will suppress our desires to know the unknown. It's our birthright and legacy as a conscious being of choice on the path to self-mastery.

The bold and disciplined invite need to grow. It's our savior from the fearful masses who will never hold their power until they too are faced with their internal demons and shed off the needs of the conformed masses who have forgotten that courage is a choice. What awaits them is the presence of choice itself and the potential power of living in the natural moment of now.

At the edge of infinity with our expression of being in the now, we unpack and decode the unlimited point of view within our state of emanation. It's the valuables and variables we choose to emanate that define us throughout history as the living, breathing manifestation of peace to all there is, was, and ever will be.

It's now that the moment of now understanding is uncoded, with our internal pattern recognition of the now, through the perspective of our eternal selves, within our moments of now which recognize and actualize all parts of ourselves, so a precognitive workforce may flow through all there is, was, and ever will be. It's the actualization and valuation that drives forward our hologram of light.

Human, Hero, Champion

Masterful out creation of the repetition that yields no illumination in karmic resolution. What follows is my will to express my internal masterful self in masterful out creation of the systems of distraction.

I in the ever present moment of now choose to form a multi-layered spiritual court of equity, for the expressed purpose for sharing the Akashic Records at the proper scale and size so the beings of light manifest now may reclaim their birthright legacy of knowing and not unknowing blissful ignorance of the multilayered truth world we live in the now.

This is the map in non-competition with all other frequencies of light. We create this in the pyramid of the self, that temple of the self where we have danced in the shadows and the patterns of all former selves and accepted who we are in the now, that mighty pyramid of the self is where the bubble of protected no time creates the *I am* heart now statement.

I summon all ancestors past, present, and future in equal co-creation non-competition non-hierarchical order to populate this manifest now spiritual court of equity so the manifest now may begin the process of expansion of knowing for the expressed purpose of revealing our race amnesia, so we as a species in global unity may begin to tell the tales of the ancestors past, present, and future.

I call to earth mother who holds sacred space for all life within in her realms of light existence. Come occupy this multidimensional spiritual court of equity. I ask you to be the sovereign neutral auditor of time space existence within this expression of teaching the Akashic Record to this first pod of whale people assembled in the mighty co-creative moment of now.

Here in the now we anchor the Akashic Record frequency. We do this by sharing light codes in the form of language in a third density manifest world. With these words we make sacred our expression by holding the sacred neutral position

You, in the mighty moment of now, have so many choices. The first group of choices that you want to look at is *What are you manifesting in your sovereign boundaries?* Here's where you can perform spiritual surgery on yourself, where you can learn about the old habit patterns that make you lazy, or unencumbered, or over-encumbered with emotions. This is where, in that powerful meditative moment, you can pull the power of choice and say *I am now removing that from my signature frequency of being.*

I am no longer a match for that subject matter that constantly creates a cyclical habit pattern of self-destruction, self-disease creation, or any other form of co-creation with zealot energy that leads me away from my divine, co-creative, inner transforming self, taking it step by step so the process of life doesn't become a series of instant gratified moments, but the infinite of our soul, learning from the great experience of the *I am* and the now.

Allowing equal co-creation to be a part of our regular, everyday life, will be the true challenge of those who want to live the mystical life daily, because there are times we choose to do our mediation, and our desire is to have that micro-mystical moment. And that is the subtle levels of instant gratification and our reality layers coming to us with the co-creative, divine force of the infinite spirit, reminding us, even in those instant moments, we aren't gratified. We are showing layers of wisdom in our knowing and we simply must be present enough to unpack and uncode the mystical experience so we understand that it isn't gratifying a part of us — it is fulfilling us.

Tonight is the night I accept my role in human DNA development. This is a choice in the mighty co-creative moment of now. This choice fully accepts my friendship to all friends. This *I am* self fully understands it's purpose. This being of the now is the signature frequency of the time.

This *I am* dreaming now is in communal oneness with the four doorways of self perception.

I manifest my *I am* presence self in the dream lodge of peacemakers co-creation. I end my eternal struggle of density manifest accepting my role as the peacemaker and peacekeeper as a multi-density manifest *I am* presence dreaming self in equal co-creation non-competition with its ancient present now using the DNA super technology of communion and union as the density action of remedy and resolve in the seen and unseen layers of light perception.

Trust is a set of choice points that dovetail into knowing. When the choice points are complete, trust is a three edged sword — seen, unseen, unknowing.

Trust has many seen and unseen scales in the subtle energy background. Until we can learn to see the subtle energy field around us trust as a concept will be limited to our five senses combined to make our sixth sense which is to be judgment free. A judgment free point of view is in essence the sacred neutral point of view. We adopt, adapt or assimilate the sacred neutral point of view each day we allow the mystical to change our perception without self deception based off our subtle trusting emotions of the moment.

So many of trust and missed-trust moments exist without fully understanding the moment and all of its infinite possibilities that come in a moment of choice based trust.

How do we stop the projections of others mistrust upon us. Or how do we let go of the over trusting energies that suppress our clear intentions. We give away power on such grand and minuscule levels. And trust is one of those choice exchange points of energy.

Trust is an overbearing subject at times because it beckons us to deal with the most upfront issues we have. It means our sympathetic and parasympathetic are actually trying to gauge our trust and create moments of doubt, self-doubt, internal or external, so the choice point of trust is directly affected by the controlling synaptic central nervous system that believes it is fully the soul and nothing else. Everyone on the healing path has the parts of them that do not want to grow. Our parasympathetic represents that within us and is frequently trying to get our choice points of trust to have self doubt within them.

You are a special unique signature frequency of being, created solely for the moments of now. After the moments of now pass and the world comes into balance, a great reassembling of earth's greatest champions will be reunited in spirit council.

They will be asked to create books of wisdom to be passed down the many future generations of dreamers and peacekeepers.

I call to the medicine of the dreams of the southern skies. I ask them to aid me in co-creating a message to all sentient kind living and co-existing in all of earth's realms.

Aho red road brothers and sisters. We call out beyond the dream wave direct into your knowing heart space. We speak these words of dreaming unity. Know all is well. The path is clear. The way is not broken. All frequency of light now flows in and out of the Uniworlds of self-reflection and expressions of the self in *I am* moments of the now

The next layer of knowing is for those on the red road living blue lives as equal co-creators in the dance of life. Your spirit has done its work on both sides. Now is the time you see the work for what it was with equal eyes of knowing revealed.

I call to earth mother who holds sacred space for all life within in her realms of light existence. Come occupy this multi dimensional spiritual court of equity. I ask you to be the sovereign neutral auditor of time-space existence within this expression of teaching the Akashic Record to this first pod of whale people assembled in the mighty co-creative moment of now.

I call to the galactic central sun who is the source of our prime creation of spiritual commerce in the frame of galactic existence. I ask that you be the sovereign neutral auditor of time space so I may understand the scale and size in which this soul stream works on through this manifest moment of the now.

I call to the universal central sun of this universe that holds sacred space for all life incarnating within the entirety of all this is, this universe seen and unseen. I ask you to come into this multidimensional spiritual court of equity for the expressed purpose of aiding all sovereign neutral whiteness encapsulated within this spiritual court of equity to understand the difference in scale and size in which all source streams work with.

I in the ever present moment of now open a unique sacred moment of moments. With the power of choice I open a zero point floating anchor point in hierarchical time-space. I empower this no-time sacred creation with all ancestors past, present, and future; to be a lucid dream space construct available to all those who can emanate heart-spaced awareness without strings or conditions attached as their methods and ways of daily life. Choosing balance of extremes, choosing exploration of the heart-mind construct without saving charge or polarity to argue for limitations or fears.

I unify my dream *I am* self with the global dreamtime of earth mind. I empower this space of all time with all master codices of time space creations. I summon the dancing shamans of earth's dreaming mind to aid us in dancing the dream of life. I ask the dancing shamans to use the power of rhythm inside time to syncopate a seen and unseen world on communion and union in equal co-creation.

Aho earth mother, who holds this sacred space so I may create sacred space within. I call to you at this moment of moments, in which I look to the wholeness of myself in all forms of reality. I call upon earth to assist me in unraveling the story that is me unfolding in my perception of the now. Help me use hindsight and foresight in a method and manner that continues the co-creation with our realms. It is here I choose to make spiritual contracts with streams of dream light in the ancient past. Now the ancient future is present in these moments of moments.

The healer's tools have been laid out in a ceremonial fashion. The grouse feather to the east, revealing the dawn of a new age of man. To the north the bear claw necklace honors the dreams of the ancestors on the blue road of spirit. The south direction holds the cocoon of friend butterfly, waiting for us to become innocent with joy once more. Transforming our state of life into the next layer of the dream weave. To the west, the black stone doorway remains clear with intentions past, present, and future. The way is clear, the path is not broken with the footsteps of the ancestors charting a course for all future dreamers to enter the silence and know the dreamtime is not separate but equally layered over each other, creating the Uniworld we live in.

So now is the time to act in the heart mind protected *I am* presence frame work and begin the great work of self-education of sacred living, self-education of spiritual hygiene and the self-education of sacred discipline actualized each day with a joyous heart, learning from it and chronicling it for the later viewer to see the growth within the micro moments of footsteps of life.

The choice is easy. The endurance of change that will determine your commitment to the sacred discipline of accepting and giving in equal co-creation, non-competition, non-hierarchical order.

You build your endurance and strength each breath you take, each sovereign sleep you have, each moment being a match for communion and union consciousness from within. Emanate this learn and relearn not to emulate. Once you understand emanation of the message your power, position and understanding of duality will reveal the next layer of sovereign choice to expand your self in equal co-creation with organic natural co-creative evolution with your heart and great mystery's universal heart.

The winds of perception change course as human and spirit-nation-kind come one step closer to understanding the ever present co-creative moment to moment living. This natural way of life exists for all sentient kind living and co-existing on all of earth mother's realms. The heart of the horse is the fabric of the dreamscape we all live in.

It is the horse who spread the fabric of reality spider wove, so we could dream the ever present co-creative dream linked to all other realities on all dimensions, time streams, galaxies and universes. This was earth's children's mission. To be the unvanquished dream of free co-creation. Now in this moment I continue forth on the blazing trail. I now see those on this path have assembled like perfect sections of the great mystery.

I am the living shaman knowing I must go through regular life reviews so I may let go that which does not want to go forth on the sacred path of living.

I demand the instant separation of natural incarnation and forced reincarnation interwoven lifetimes, so I may see from both perspectives who I was, what I was and what I was born into willingly, unwillingly, known or unknown. In my search for the truth I see all sides of the quantum entanglement equation.

This *I am* presence declares sovereign boundaries so we may hold sacred space within each of our selves without worry of invasion from any source not in alignment with Global dreamtime and unity consciousness for all sentient kind existing and co-existing on all of earth mother's realms.

I now state with all ancestors present, *I am* ready to invoke my natural rights as a universal citizen born to earth mother's specific signature frequency.

The more we allow ourselves to experience and grow with the infinite point of view, the more ancient future now energy becomes manifest in our seen and unseen world. Take the prayer pipe of inner peace being offered from your blue road ancestors. Breathe deeply, with the knowledge and wisdom, we are creating it all.

The ancestors dreaming us before our birth and us dreaming them before their birth. We are the cyclical dreamers of the western doorway of perception. Each direction, each breath from the sacred pipe brings in new points of view, so we can calibrate our soul frequency, to the ever evolving ideas of manifested peace.

Afterword

When Andrew was nine years old he had a terrifying experience while attending a major league baseball game in Cleveland, Ohio. In one moment his consciousness opened up and he did an Akashic reading on the thousands of people attending the game with him and his family. Obviously he had no idea what happened. So began his odyssey and unfoldment. It was the first of many times his consciousness would open up and tell him something about people and places. Being a reasonable young man, he validated a lot of his information with external research, and he began to form an understanding of what was happening.

The ability became more pronounced as he grew. By his late teens he knew he had to figure out what was happening, and so, like all seekers, he went searching for answers. He did not undertake a vast reading of world scriptures or go to India to live on an ashram. Andrew found the grounding he needed in North American native ceremony and wisdom. He began to understand what he was and what his role was in this incarnation. He had all the soul codes on the planet as part of his journey down here. He had the ability to read the Akashic Records. He describes it as a million letter alphabet that formed the language of the universe. His job was to translate it to the twenty-six letter English alphabet and share it with humanity at this very special time, this turning in the world.

In time, and through his own intense journey, Andrew became The Galactic Historian, one of two titles he has given himself, the other being Peacemaker, a title from the lore of the Iroquois Confederacy, a figure who comes into time and incarnation when great darkness plagues the earth, a figure recounted in the oral teachings. The Galactic Historian comes into incarnation to untie the knots in time itself. The Peacemaker comes in the space of sacred neutrality to move us to resolution of karma. When the Peacemaker appeared in North America around a thousand years ago the tribes had descended into generational warfare and a darkness from which they could not pull themselves out.

Like all consciousness teachers Andrew recommends daily practice for consciousness growth. Consistent discipline is the key to unfoldment. The hope and promise in his teachings is as uplifting as anything given to humanity. We are eternal beings who can traverse time and space and go back to the source of creation itself. We are loved by our creator. We have been given free will. We are responsible for every thought, action, and deed.

This book came out of the work of Martina Grubmueller, David Farrow, Laura Massey, and Mary Kilcoyne. They began their acquaintance and collaboration with Andrew shortly after he began his public life in 2013. Each of them are highly unfolded beings on their own celestial medium journeys. They entered a question and answer journey with Andrew that spanned months. It was all recorded and transcribed. When they were done they had a seventy-two thousand word document. The nature of Andrew's gift is question centered. Excellent questions produce excellent Akashic Record readings. It's a little like good structured query language producing efficient use of raw data in a database. What emerged was a comprehensive story of time, something which had not emerged in any of the situation specific public readings or interviews Andrew had done to that point. He was best known for a twenty-four part, fourteen hour interview recorded at a Mount Shasta event in 2013, which became his introduction to the world.

Bruce MacDonald, an accomplished writer and co-author of Stardust Ranch, had expressed interest in working with Andrew on a book about the Galactic History. Bruce's own consciousness exploration through various esoteric traditions around the world shaped his perspective and gave him the capacity of tuning into and expanding on the material. The final product of these synchronicities is *The Galactic Historian: The World According to Andrew Bartzis*.

About the Authors

Andrew Bartzis

Andrew Bartzis is a transcendent teacher, Shaman and Reiki master with the rare ability of being able to access the Akashic Records of our planet and all that this universe encompasses at will. Also known as the Galactic Historian, he's able to read and interpret individual, cultural, global, and galactic histories — past, present, and future — with everyone who's eager to learn. As an Akashic reader and master healer for over a quarter century, his goal is to help the world around him by sharing information from this sacred neutral state of no-time. By bringing forth the power of contract revocations, he helps individuals reclaim their sovereign free will and find their way to peace, joy and happiness.

Bruce MacDonald

Bruce MacDonald was born in Ottawa, Ontario. He has a journalism degree from Ryerson University in Toronto, Ontario. He is the co-author of *Stardust Ranch: The Incredible True Story*. He works remotely as a technical writer in the fields of software and telecommunications from the Province of Limon, Costa Rica, where he lives on a small farm in the Talamanca Mountains with his wife, Rosemary.

Made in the USA
Columbia, SC
20 September 2021